#1

WINDSOR HOUSE SCHOOL
2132 HAMILTON AVENUE
NORTH VANCOUVER, BC
V7P 3M3

ADDISON-WESLEY

QUEST 2000

EXPLORING MATHEMATICS

AUTHORS

Ricki Wortzman   Lalie Harcourt   Brendan Kelly   Peggy Morrow
Randall I. Charles   David C. Brummett   Carne S. Barnett

CONTRIBUTING AUTHORS

Linda Beatty   Anne Boyd   Fred Crouse   Susan Gordon
Elisabeth Javor   Alma Ramirez   Freddie Lee Renfro   Mary M. Soniat-Thompson

REVISED EDITION

Addison-Wesley Publishers Limited

Don Mills, Ontario • Reading, Massachusetts • Menlo Park, California
New York • Wokingham, England • Amsterdam • Bonn
Sydney • Singapore • Tokyo • Madrid • San Juan • Paris
Seoul • Milan • Mexico City • Taipei

Reviewers/Consultants

Marie Beckberger, Springfield Public School, Mississauga, Ontario
Jan Carruthers, Somerset and District Elementary School, King's County, Nova Scotia
Garry Garbolinsky, Tanner's Crossing School, Minnedosa, Manitoba
Darlene Hayes, King Edward Community School, Winnipeg, Manitoba
Barbara Hunt, Bayview Hill Elementary School, Richmond Hill, Ontario
Rita Janes, Roman Catholic School Board, St. John's, Newfoundland
Karen McClelland, Oak Ridges Public School, Richmond Hill, Ontario
Betty Morris, Edmonton Catholic School District #7, Edmonton, Alberta
Jeanette Mumford, Early Childhood Multicultural Services, Vancouver, B.C.
Evelyn Sawicki, Calgary Roman Catholic Separate School District #1, Calgary, Alberta
Darlene Shandola, Thomas Kidd Elementary School, Richmond, B.C.
Elizabeth Sloane, Dewson Public School, Toronto, Ontario
Denise White, Morrish Public School, Scarborough, Ontario
Elizabeth Wylie, Clark Boulevard Public School, Brampton, Ontario

Technology Advisors

Fred Crouse, Centreville, Nova Scotia; Flick Douglas, North York, Ontario; Cynthia Dunham, Framingham, MA; Susan Seidman, Toronto, Ontario; Evelyn J. Woldman, Framingham, MA; Diana Nunnaley, Maynard, MA

Editorial Development: Susan Petersiel Berg, Margaret Cameron, Mei Lin Cheung, Lesley Haynes, Anita Smale Fran Cohen/First Folio Resource Group, Inc., Lynne Gulliver, Louise MacKenzie, Helen Nolan, Mary Reeve

Design: McClanahan & Company
Wycliffe Smith Design

Cover Design: The Pushpin Group

Canadian Cataloguing in Publication Data

Wortzman, Ricki
Quest 2000 : exploring mathematics, grade 6,
revised edition: student book

First and third authors in reverse order on
previous ed.
ISBN 0-201-55275-2

I. Mathematics – Juvenile literature.   I. Harcourt,
Lalie, 1951– .   II. Kelly, B. (Brendan), 1943– .
III. Title.

QA107.K45   1996   510   C95-932758-4

Pearson Education Canada.

ISBN 0-201-55275-2

This book contains recycled product and is acid free.

Printed and bound in Canada

10 11 ITIB 03 02 01

Table of Contents

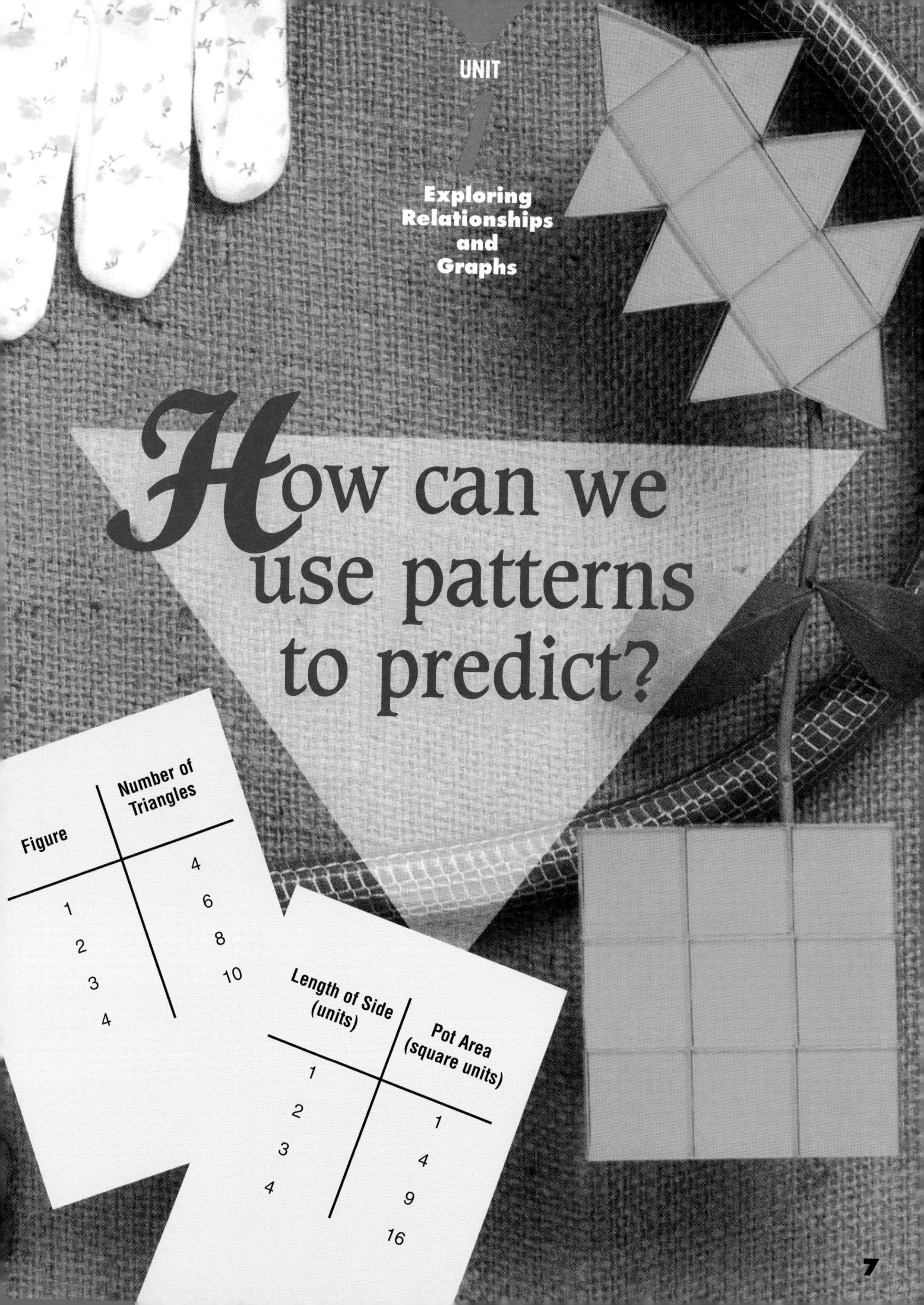

UNIT 1

Exploring Relationships and Graphs

How can we use patterns to predict?

Figure	Number of Triangles
1	4
2	6
3	8
4	10

Length of Side (units)	Pot Area (square units)
1	1
2	4
3	9
4	16

**EXPLORING RELATIONSHIPS
AND GRAPHS**

S·T·A·R·T·I·N·G OUT

Kevin's Grade	Alice's Age
6	4
7	5
8	6
9	7
?	?
?	?
?	?

Kevin uses a pattern. He predicts how old his sister will be during each of his school grades.

Graph of Time and Distance Travelled

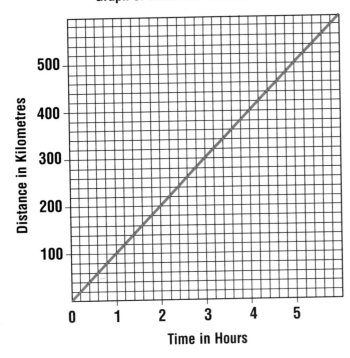

Ms. Meeker uses the patterns in a graph. She predicts how far she can travel if she drives at the speed limit.

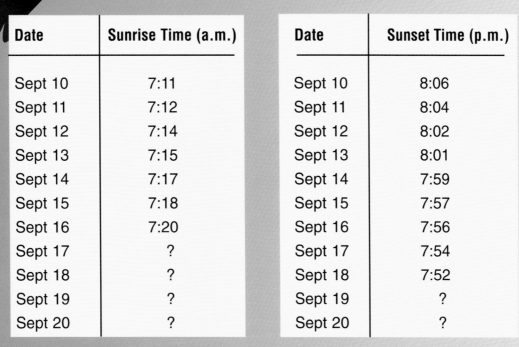

Date	Sunrise Time (a.m.)
Sept 10	7:11
Sept 11	7:12
Sept 12	7:14
Sept 13	7:15
Sept 14	7:17
Sept 15	7:18
Sept 16	7:20
Sept 17	?
Sept 18	?
Sept 19	?
Sept 20	?

Date	Sunset Time (p.m.)
Sept 10	8:06
Sept 11	8:04
Sept 12	8:02
Sept 13	8:01
Sept 14	7:59
Sept 15	7:57
Sept 16	7:56
Sept 17	7:54
Sept 18	7:52
Sept 19	?
Sept 20	?

Una uses a pattern. She predicts what time the sun will rise and set each day in Vancouver.

1 a. What is the rule for each pattern shown here and on page 8?

b. Use the rule for each pattern. Extend the T-tables with at least three more entries.

c. What other patterns can you think of that are like the ones here?

My Journal: When do you use number patterns in your daily activities?

STARTING OUT

Year	First-Class Postage
1910	2¢
1920	3¢
1930	2¢
1940	3¢
1950	4¢
1960	5¢
1970	6¢
1980	17¢
1990	39¢

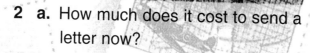

2 a. How much does it cost to send a letter now?

b. What do you think it will cost to send a first-class letter in the year 2010? Explain your thinking.

c. What information would you like to know to help you predict?

d. What other times have you seen data that have no pattern?

My Journal: What do you know about patterns? What do you still want to learn?

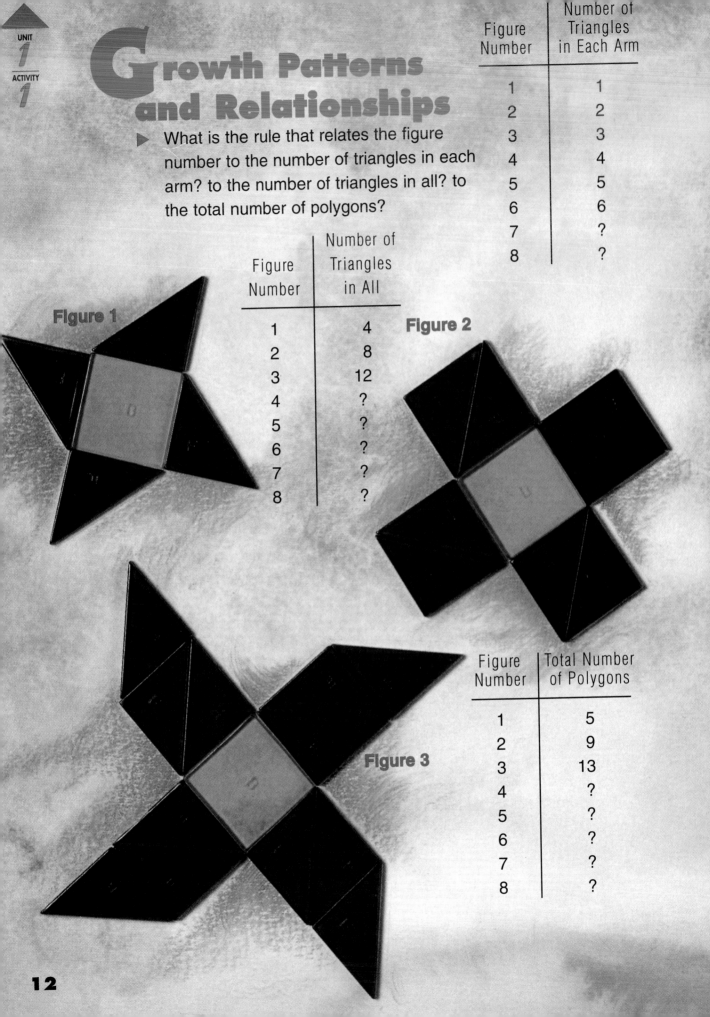

Growth Patterns and Relationships

▶ What is the rule that relates the figure number to the number of triangles in each arm? to the number of triangles in all? to the total number of polygons?

Figure Number	Number of Triangles in Each Arm
1	1
2	2
3	3
4	4
5	5
6	6
7	?
8	?

Figure 1

Figure 2

Figure Number	Number of Triangles in All
1	4
2	8
3	12
4	?
5	?
6	?
7	?
8	?

Figure 3

Figure Number	Total Number of Polygons
1	5
2	9
3	13
4	?
5	?
6	?
7	?
8	?

12

Growing Trees

▶ What is the rule that relates the figure number of the tree to the number of triangles? to the number of squares? to the total number of polygons?

Figure Number	Total Number of Polygons
1	5
2	8
3	11
4	?
5	?
6	?

Figure Number	Number of Squares
1	3
2	4
3	5
4	?
5	?
6	?

Figure Number	Number of Triangles
1	2
2	4
3	6
4	?
5	?
6	?

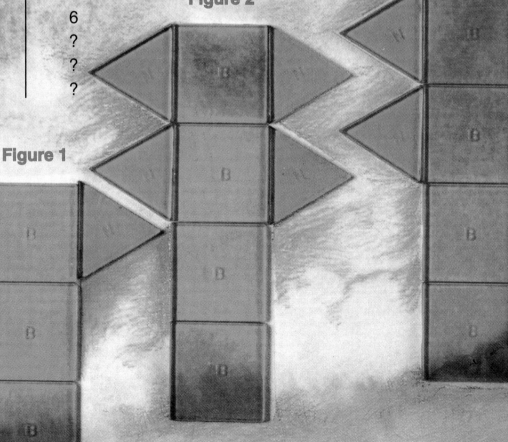

Figure 1

Figure 2

Figure 3

Flying Kites

▷ What is the rule that relates the figure number of the kite to the number of triangles? to the number of rhombuses? to the total number of polygons?

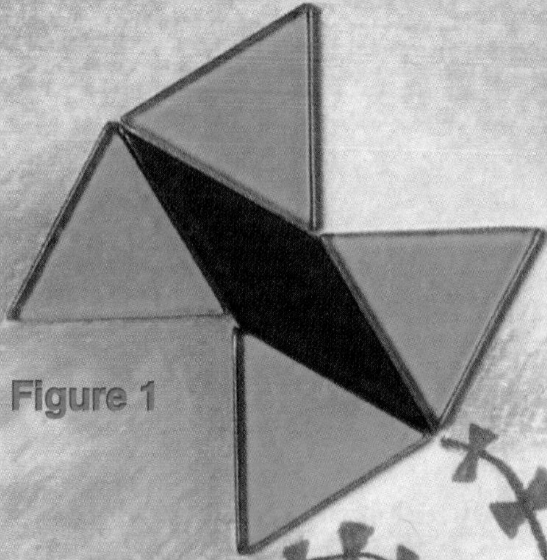

Figure 2

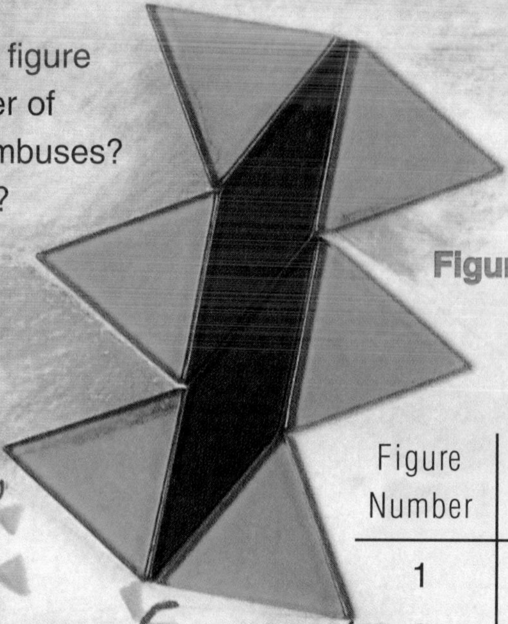

Figure 1

Figure Number	Number of Triangles
1	4
2	6
3	8
4	?
5	?
6	?

Figure Number	Number of Rhombuses
1	1
2	2
3	3
4	?
5	?
6	?

Figure 3

Figure Number	Total Number of Polygons
1	5
2	8
3	11
4	?
5	?
6	?

1. Draw the next two figures in this sequence. Write the rule. Use the rule to complete the T-table.

Figure 1

Figure 2

Figure Number	Number of Triangles
1	3
2	5
3	7
4	?
5	?
6	?

2. Create a T-table that follows the rule "multiply by a number, then add a number." Challenge a classmate to find your rule.

3. *My Journal:* How can you use data from a T-table to discover a rule?

Practise *Your Skills*

Use the tables. Write a rule that relates each output number to each input number. Copy and complete each table using your rule.

1.

Input	Output
0	0
3	9
7	21
10	30
12	?
15	?
20	?

2.

Input	Output
0	4
8	12
11	15
14	18
20	?
35	?
45	?

Graphing Perimeters and Areas of Squares

The numbers in a T-table can be written as **ordered pairs.**

First Number	Second Number		Ordered Pair
0	2	⟶	(0, 2)
1	3	⟶	(1, 3)
2	4	⟶	(2, 4)
3	5	⟶	(3, 5)
4	6	⟶	(4, 6)
5	7	⟶	(5, 7)

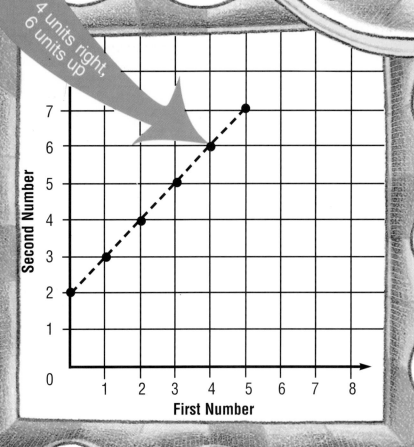

4 units right, 6 units up

Ordered pairs from a T-table can be plotted as points on a coordinate grid.

The first number represents the horizontal distance from the origin. The second number represents the vertical distance from the origin.

▶ How is the **perimeter** of a square related to the length of its side?

▶ How is the **area** of a square related to the length of its side?

Side length (cm)	Perimeter (cm)	Ordered Pair
0	0	(0, 0)
1	4	(1, 4)
2	8	(2, 8)
3	12	?
4	?	?
5	?	?

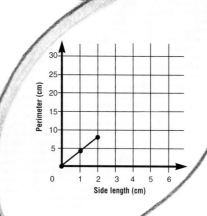

Side length (cm)	Area (cm^2)	Ordered Pair
0	0	(0, 0)
1	1	(1, 1)
2	4	(2, 4)
3	9	?
4	?	?

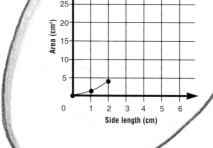

The vertical and horizontal axes may use different scales.

▶ What patterns do you see?

ON YOUR OWN

1. Copy and complete the T-table for the design below. Then write ordered pairs. Plot the ordered pairs as points on a coordinate grid.

Triangles	Squares
1	3
2	6
3	9
4	12
5	?
6	?

2. How many squares would you need for 15 triangles?

3. *My Journal:* What have you learned about graphing ordered pairs from a T-table?

Practise Your Skills

1. Make a graph by plotting these ordered pairs on a coordinate grid.
(1, 2) (2, 4) (3, 6) (4, 8) (5, 10) (6, 12)

2. Write the ordered pairs that are plotted on this graph.

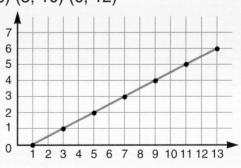

Bits & Bar Codes

Have you ever wondered how computers process information? Computers are electronic. Imagine a system of switches that is either on or off.

ON 1 OFF 0 OFF 0 ON 1 OFF 0

These switches can be represented with the binary numbers, 0 and 1. In a binary or base-two number system, there are only two digits, 0 and 1. These digits are called *bits* for short. Numbers greater than 0 or 1 can be written as binary numbers and represented by series of bits. Like the base ten number system you use, the binary number system has place values. To read a binary number, you need to know the value of each place.

Bar codes like this one are read by an infrared scanner. A detector converts the infrared light from the bar code into binary numbers, which a computer can process.

9 780201 840049

Base Ten Number	Binary Place Value				
	16s	8s	4s	2s	1s
0					0
1					1
2				1	0
3				1	1
4			1	0	0
5			1	0	1
8		1	0	0	0
10		1	0	1	0
11		1	0	1	1
13		1	1	0	1
14		1	1	1	0
15		1	1	1	1
16	1	0	0	0	0

1. What patterns do you see in the binary table? How are the numbers 2, 4, 8, and 16 represented? What do they have in common? How would 32 be represented?

2. How would you represent 26? Explain your reasoning.

3. Where have you seen bar codes used? (Hint: You are probably holding a bar code in your hand right now.) Why do you think it is important for computers to interpret the information from bar codes?

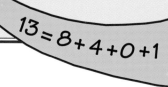

13 = 8 + 4 + 0 + 1

Multiple Representations of Patterns

Match Up

1. Find four matching sets. Each set must contain a drawing, a rule, a T-table, and a graph.

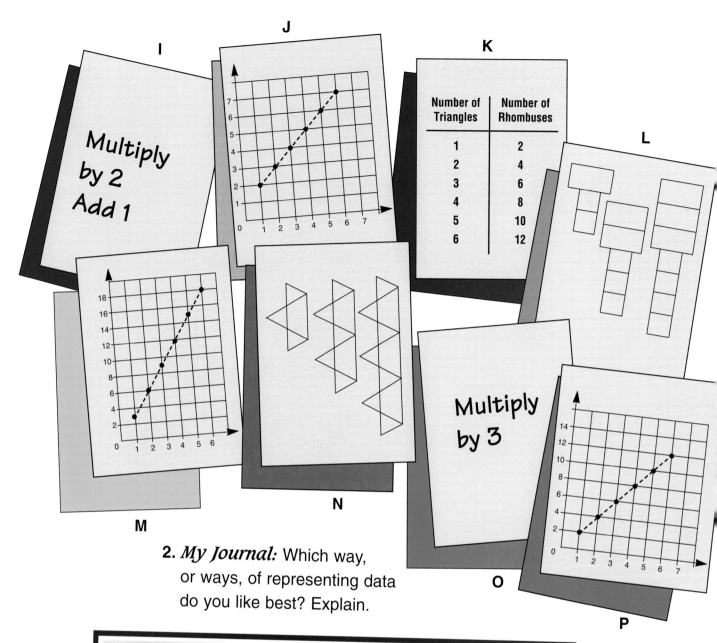

I Multiply by 2 Add 1

K

Number of Triangles	Number of Rhombuses
1	2
2	4
3	6
4	8
5	10
6	12

O Multiply by 3

2. *My Journal:* Which way, or ways, of representing data do you like best? Explain.

Practise Your Skills

Write a rule for each T-table. The rule relates the number in column A to the number in column B.

1.	A	B
	1	3
	2	5
	3	7
	4	9

2.	A	B
	1	4
	2	8
	3	12
	4	16

3.	A	B
	1	1
	2	4
	3	9
	4	16

Related Rules

Suppose a 2-m tree has 3 coconuts,
a 3-m tree has 5 coconuts, and
a 4-m tree has 7 coconuts.

▶ Suppose this pattern continues. How
many coconuts will a 10-m tree have?

Tree Table

Height (metres)	Number of Coconuts
2	3
3	5
4	7
5	?
6	?
7	?

Day	Total Coconuts Eaten
1	3
2	6
3	9
4	12

A monkey eats 3 coconuts a day. Continue the table.
Draw a graph for the total number of coconuts eaten by
the end of each day through day 10.

▶ How does the graph differ if the monkey eats
5 coconuts a day? 11 coconuts a day?

Some mysterious plants grow very quickly. A botanist recorded these data from three different plants.

Plant A	
Day	Height (cm)
1	3
2	4
3	5
4	6

Plant B	
Day	Height (cm)
1	4
2	5
3	6
4	7

Plant C	
Day	Height (cm)
1	6
2	7
3	8
4	9

Another group of plants provided these data.

Plant D	
Day	Height (cm)
1	1
2	3
3	5
4	7
5	9

Plant E	
Day	Height (cm)
1	5
2	8
3	11
4	14
5	17

Plant F	
Day	Height (cm)
1	7
2	12
3	17
4	22
5	27

▶ What is the growth rule for each plant?
What do the graphs look like?
What would each plant's height be on day 10?

ON
YOUR
OWN

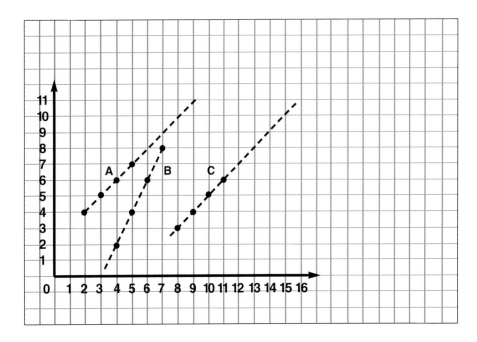

1. Make a T-table for each of graphs A, B, and C. Then write a rule for each relationship in your own words.

2. Write a rule of your own. Make a T-table for your rule. Show at least six rows in your table.

3. *My Journal:* What have you learned about writing a rule for a graph?

Practise Your Skills

Write a rule for each T-table. Some rules involve two operations.

1.

Quantity 1	Quantity 2
9	7
13	11
6	4
3	1
5	3
8	6

2.

Quantity 1	Quantity 2
8	21
2	3
4	9
10	27
7	18
6	15

3.

Quantity 1	Quantity 2
1	7
9	23
3	11
4	13
12	29
15	35

In each T-table, find the pair of numbers that does not follow the rule.

4. Add 5

Quantity 1	Quantity 2
7	12
9	15
12	17
3	8
21	26
18	23

5. Multiply by 3, add 1

Quantity 1	Quantity 2
1	4
9	28
10	31
15	45
6	19
5	16

6. Multiply by 4, subtract 2

Quantity 1	Quantity 2
10	38
4	14
7	26
2	6
11	42
9	32

Finding Rules

Examine the number sets above the lines.

▶ What is the rule for each set that relates the first two columns to the third?

Find the number sets below each line that follow the rule.

1.

3	2	5
1	4	3
6	2	11
5	3	14
8	2	15

10	2	19
4	6	23
1	3	1

2.

2	3	10
5	2	14
1	3	7
8	2	20
1	1	5

3	0	4
2	5	12
7	1	11

3.

10	5	3
8	4	3
14	7	3
12	4	4
15	5	4

9	3	3
16	4	5
18	6	4

4.

20	2	9
15	5	2
8	8	0
27	3	8
7	1	6

20	4	4
17	1	16
24	8	4

ON YOUR OWN

▶ Find the rule for each set. The rule relates the first two columns to the third.

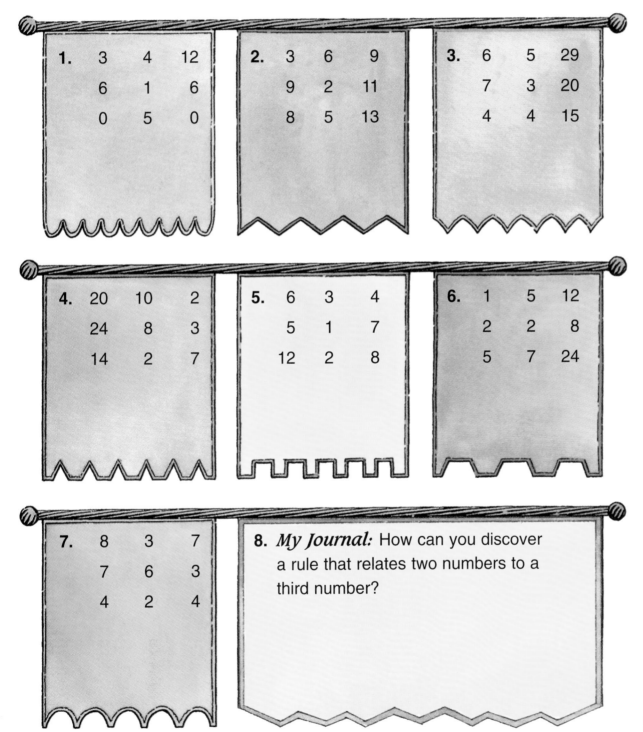

1.
3	4	12
6	1	6
0	5	0

2.
3	6	9
9	2	11
8	5	13

3.
6	5	29
7	3	20
4	4	15

4.
20	10	2
24	8	3
14	2	7

5.
6	3	4
5	1	7
12	2	8

6.
1	5	12
2	2	8
5	7	24

7.
8	3	7
7	6	3
4	2	4

8. *My Journal:* How can you discover a rule that relates two numbers to a third number?

27

A SOUP-ER ROLLER DERBY

You can conduct an experiment. See how increasing the number of cubes in a can affects the distance the can rolls.

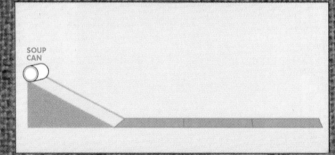

SOUP CAN

The diagram above shows one set-up. Use a similar set-up or invent your own.

Use your set-up to do an experiment. Create a data table, a graph, and a rule.

- How far does an empty can roll?
- How far does the can containing different numbers of cubes roll?
- What predictions can you make?
- How else could you find a relationship between number of cubes and distance a can rolls?

*C*heck **Y**OURSELF

Great job! You conducted an experiment to find a relationship between the number of cubes in a can and the distance the can rolls. Your plans, data, predictions, and results were clearly written. You used a table, a graph, and a rule to show your results. You wrote to explain how the table, graph, and rule are related.

PROBLEM BANK

1. a. Each pane of glass in a window is one metre square. The moulding around each pane must be painted. Complete the T-table for numbers of panes from 4 to 8. Show the length of moulding that must be painted for windows with each number of panes shown. What pattern do you see? Describe it and the rule you are using.

Window	Number of Panes	Length of Moulding in Metres
	1	4
	2	7
	3	10
	•	•
	•	•
	•	•
	8	?

b. Draw a graph. Show the length of moulding corresponding to the number of panes in each window.

c. What length of moulding would frame a window with ten panes? How did you decide?

2. a. Look at the T-table. What rule do you discover?

b. Continue the table. Figure out the price of an article whose cost with G.S.T. is $7.49.

c. Use the rule. Figure out the cost, after G.S.T., of an article priced at $12.00.

Price	Cost with G.S.T. Included
$1.00	$1.07
$2.00	$2.14
$3.00	$3.21
$4.00	$4.28

3. When a publisher ships multiple copies of its mathematics book, it records the total mass of the package. To help the shipper figure out the mass of each package, this graph is posted. It shows the mass for each number of books shipped.

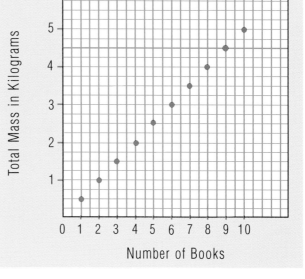

Total Mass in Kilograms

Number of Books

   a. Make a T-table. Show the mass of a package containing one book, two books, three books, and so on up to ten books.

   b. Describe any patterns you can find in the T-table. Use the T-table. Predict the mass of a package containing 15 books.

4. Find the rule for each set. The rule relates the first two columns to the third, or the first three columns to the fourth.

   a. 2 6 12
       0 7 0
       2 3 6

   b. 2 3 2 10
       4 1 7 35
       8 0 1 8

   c. 18 6 3
       30 5 6
       25 5 5

5. Complete each T-table. Write the rule that relates Quantity 1 in each table to Quantity 2 in each table. Each rule involves two operations.

a.

Quantity 1	Quantity 2
3	1
4	3
5	5
6	7
?	?
?	?
?	?

b.

Quantity 1	Quantity 2
6	23
8	31
10	39
12	47
?	?
?	?
?	?

c.

Quantity 1	Quantity 2
1	4
2	7
3	12
4	19
?	?
?	?
?	?

Number of Copies	Cost ¢
1	15
2	20
3	25
4	30
5	35
6	40

1. This T-table shows the cost of making photocopies.

    a. What is the cost of making ten copies?

    b. Graph the data.

2. Toothpicks are used to create small triangles.

    a. Continue the T-table. Show the number of toothpicks needed for eight triangles.

    b. Write the numbers in the T-table as ordered pairs.

    c. Graph the ordered pairs.

Number of Small Triangles	Number of Toothpicks
1	3
2	5
3	7

3. Create a T-table with the rule "multiply by 2, add 2."

4. Write the next three rows for each T-table. Write a rule for each table.

a.

A	B
1	5
2	6
3	7
4	8

b.

A	B
2	4
3	6
4	8
5	10

c.

A	B
13	10
12	9
11	8
10	7

5. Write four sets of numbers that follow each rule.
   a. multiply the first number by the second to get the third
   b. multiply the first number by 2, then subtract the second to get the third

6. Find the rule for each set. The rule relates the first two columns to the third.

a.

1	4	5
8	7	15
7	19	26
2	5	7

b.

1	3	5
2	3	8
4	2	10
6	5	32

7. This graph shows the distance travelled by a car for each hour travelling time.
   a. Copy and complete the T-table for the graph.
   b. Predict how far the car will travel in 8 hours.

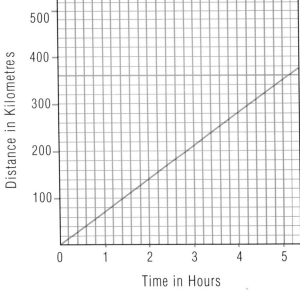

Travelling Time (h)	Distance Travelled (km)
1	?
2	?
3	?
4	?

Population
of Calgary
0.7 million

CANADA 43

Post Card

Ziba Wilso
206 10th St.
Edmonton, A
T

...ved the stampede
and the Saddledome
is great — come with
me next time!
Your friend,
Liz

Ian Crysler Photography
Calgary, Alberta, Canada

beads 0.7 cm
I

Only 500 attend
movie premier.

Record 500 fit on
giant chuckwagon!

VOL. NO 549 The Local Gazette
• • • • • • • • First Edition • • • • • • • • •

The New Budget
$250 Million

City officials met late yesterday to
approve a final budget of $250 mil-
lion for the city libraries. Although
...dget was not as large as
...ry officials were
...itional

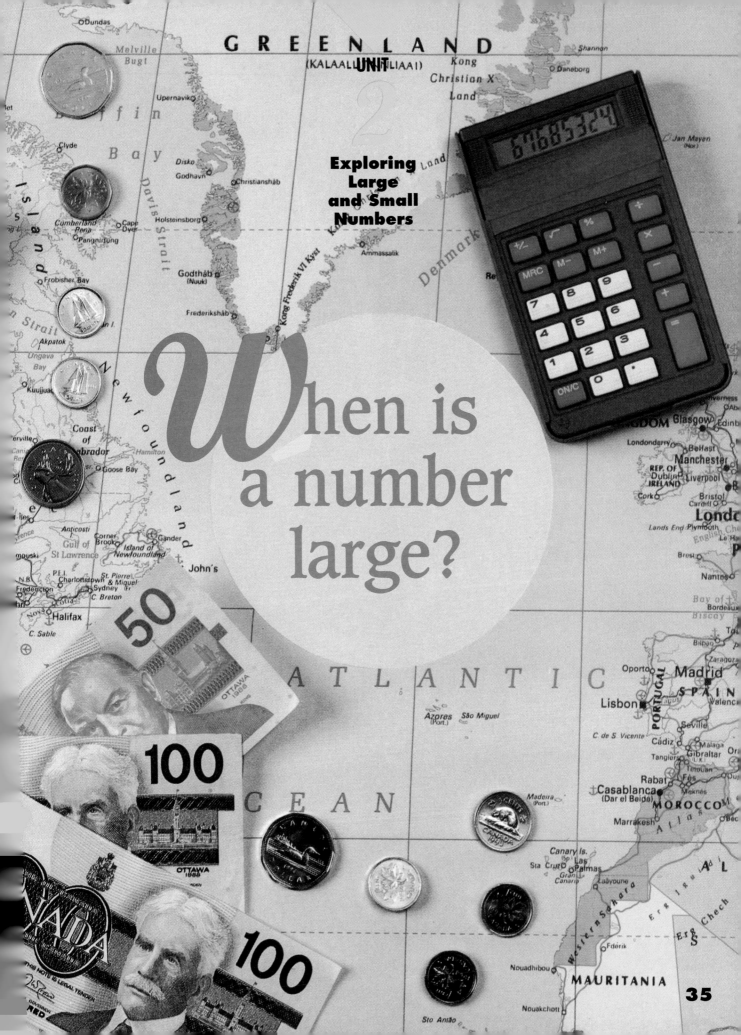

GREENLAND
(KALAALLIT NUNAAT)

**Exploring
Large
and Small
Numbers**

When is a number large?

EXPLORING LARGE
AND SMALL NUMBERS

S·T·A·R·T·I·N·G
S OUT

The world's largest and fanciest jewelled egg — the Argyle Library Egg — stands 70 cm tall. It was designed by a London jeweller. It took six craftspeople 7000 hours to create. The egg was made from 16.8 kg of gold and studded with 20 000 pink diamonds. And get ready for the price tag — about $14 000 000!

1 a. How are numbers used to describe the egg?

b. Draw a special egg that is smaller than the one described here. Use numbers to describe it.

c. Draw an egg that would break the record set by the one shown here. Use numbers to describe it.

My Journal: What does it mean to compare numbers?

EXPLORING LARGE
AND SMALL NUMBERS

S·T·A·R·T·I·N·G

OUT

2 **a.** About how many times as great as the mass of the white-tailed deer is the mass of the walrus? Explain your thinking.

   b. Which animal has a mass about 1000 times as great as the pine marten? Explain your choice.

   c. Write as many statements as you can to compare the masses of these animals.

Walrus 1005 kg

Pine marten 1 kg

River otter 10 kg

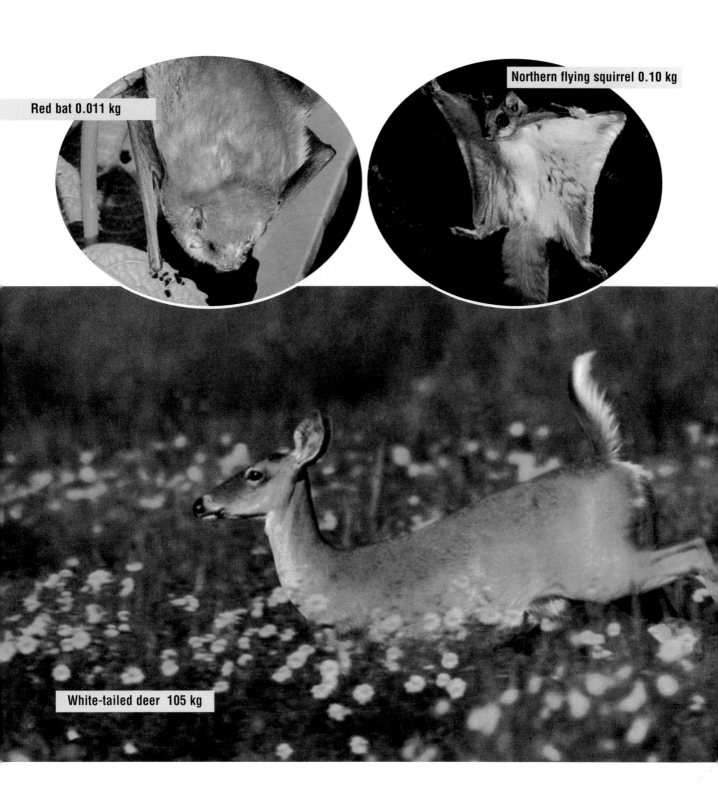

Red bat 0.011 kg

Northern flying squirrel 0.10 kg

White-tailed deer 105 kg

My Journal: What do you know about the relationship
between 10 and 100? between 100 and 1000?
between 1000 and 100 000?

Understanding Large Numbers

Imagine you had one of these annual salaries after taxes.

$1 000 000

$75 000

$17 000

$850 000

$300 000

$100 000

$40 000

$5 000 000

Didn't we almost have it all?

How will you spend your imaginary salary?

Year-round home	$200 000
Luxury home	$900 000
Season ticket to the ballet	$1 000
Vacation home	$125 000
Yacht	$1 750 000
Caribbean trip	$3 000
Sailboat	$19 000
Stereo/video system	$6 000
Speedboat	$34 000
Recreational vehicle	$55 000
Trip to the World Series	$2 000
Sports car	$32 000
Luxury car	$63 000
Fully equipped gym	$5 500
Yearly rent	$9 000
Minivan	$25 000
Motorcycle	$7 300
Food for one year	$3 700
Mountain bike	$750
Swimming pool	$11 000
Cruise	$8 000
Round-the-world cruise	$47 000
New clothes	$2 000
European vacation	$4 800
Diamond necklace	$390 000
Computer	$2 800
Diamond watch	$24 000

MEET Some Wealthy People

I'll Be Back

Who they are	What they do	Earnings in a recent year
Michael Eisner	Head of Disney	$202 000 000
Steven Spielberg	Film director	$32 000 000
Charles Schulz	Cartoonist	$31 000 000
Eddie Murphy	Actor	$31 000 000
Arnold Schwarzenegger	Actor	$22 000 000
Oprah Winfrey	Television host	$21 000 000
Whitney Houston	Singer	$15 000 000
Jack Nicholson	Actor	$11 000 000
Doug Gilmour	Hockey player	$3 000 000
Jim Abbott	Baseball player	$2 800 000

MEET some REALLY Wealthy people

Who they are	How they earned their fortune	Estimate of their worth
Taikichiro Mori	Tokyo real estate	$18 000 000 000
Sultan of Brunei	Oil production	$14 000 000 000
William Gates	Computer software	$12 000 000 000
Queen Elizabeth II	Inheritance	$6 000 000 000
Bronfman family	Real estate	$4 900 000 000
Irving family	Oil	$3 700 000 000

ON YOUR OWN

▶ Use the data on page 41.

1. About how many times as great as the earnings of Doug Gilmour are the earnings of Steven Spielberg?

2. About how many times as great as the earnings of Whitney Houston are the earnings of Michael Eisner?

3. Which person on the first list earned close to $\frac{1}{1000}$ of the estimated worth of William Gates?

4. *My Journal:* What have you learned about the relationship between one million and one billion?

Doug Gilmour

Practise Your Skills

1. Write the number that is:
- **a.** 1000 times as great as 100
- **b.** 1000 times as great as 1000
- **c.** 1000 times as great as 1 000 000

2. Write > or < for each ■.
- **a.** 452 693 ■ 831 026
- **b.** 43 774 ■ 43 747
- **c.** 158 691 ■ 27 384
- **d.** 770 509 ■ 75 241

Representing Numbers

▶ Find the numbers. Compare how they are written.

Mathematicians have used a computer to calculate the number π (pi) to 2 260 321 336 places. This is more precise than the commonly used 3.14, which is rounded to two decimal places. In fact, the computer printout would be thousands of pages long.

The favourite North American snack is the potato chip. Sales in a recent year were $4.3 billion.

Scientists believe there are 6500 objects orbiting Earth. Some are satellites still in use, but most of the objects are no longer functioning.

A balance scale has been built that can measure the mass of an object to one hundred millionth of a gram (0.000 000 01 g).

Math Gazette

A list of the top 10 money-earning movies of all time showed that Steven Spielberg was the most successful director, with four films:

Movie	Millions
Jaws	$458.0
Indiana Jones and the Last Crusade	$494.8
E.T.	$701.1
Jurassic Park	$860.0

Mathematicians broke a code that is based on the following number:
114 381 625 757 888 867 669 235 779 976 146 612 010 218 296 721 242 362 562 561 842 935 706 935 245 733 897 830 597 123 563 958 705 058 989 075 147 599 290 026 879 543 541.

The code number, which protects a security system, is the product of two factors, each a prime number. Developers of the code expected it to take 40 quadrillion years to find the pair of factors. Mathematicians and computers took 17 years to break the code.

According to a report by NASA, the average astronaut uses about 4.5 kg of supplies every day. These include 0.6 kg of food, 2.8 kg of water, and 0.8 kg of oxygen. Storage and costs are both problems: it costs about $11 000 per kilogram to ship supplies into space.

Want to put money to work for you? Suppose you invest $1000 in a retirement savings plan when you are 25. It has a real return of 4% (interest rate minus inflation rate). Your investment will be worth $4801 when you are 65. If you invest $1000 each year for those 40 years, you'll have $98 827! That's the beauty of earning interest!

▶ Record the greater number in each pair. Explain how you decided.

1. 4.25 million or 24.3 thousand

2. 2.5 billion or 8345 million

3. 0.9 billion or 999 999 999

4. 5.3 million or 57.8 thousand

▶ Read each headline. Do you think each number is exact or rounded? Explain how you decided.

5.
Budget for Next Year to be $15 Billion

6.
Company Sells One Millionth Minivan

7.
Record Attendance— 53 124 See Close Game

8.
My Journal: Write some newspaper headlines that show what you have learned about writing one number in different ways.

Practise Your Skills

1. Rewrite each number using standard form.
   a. 12 million   **b.** 4.25 million
   c. 5.3 billion   **d.** 62.5 million

2. Write a rounded number for each number.
   a. 129 967   **b.** 408 381   **c.** 1 003 794
   d. 989 786   **e.** 24 267 991   **f.** 8 981 967

Patterns in Numbers

This chart shows some ways to write powers of 10.

▶ Copy and complete the chart.

Pattern Activity 1

millions	hundred thousands	ten thousands	thousands	hundreds	tens	ones	tenths	hundredths	thousandths	ten thousandths	hundred thousandths	millionths
?	?	10 000	1000	100	10	1	0.1	0.01	0.001	0.0001	?	?
?	?	?	10 x 10 x 10	10 x 10	10	1	$\frac{1}{10}$	$\frac{1}{10 \times 10}$	$\frac{1}{10 \times 10 \times 10}$	?	?	?
?	?	?	10^3	10^2	10^1	10^0	$\frac{1}{10^1}$	$\frac{1}{10^2}$	$\frac{1}{10^3}$	?	?	?

This chart shows what happens to 14 when you multiply it by powers of 10.

▶ What patterns do you see?

Pattern Activity 2

Millions			Thousands			Units			
Hundreds	Tens	Ones	Hundreds	Tens	Ones	Hundreds	Tens	Ones	
						1	4	0	14 x 10
					1	4	0	0	14 x 100
				1	4	0	0	0	14 x 1000
			1	4	0	0	0	0	14 x 10 000
		1	4	0	0	0	0	0	14 x 100 000
	1	4	0	0	0	0	0	0	14 x 1 000 000

▶ Make charts like the one above for these numbers.

1. 9   **2.** 17   **3.** 106

1. Suppose you wrote one number per second and never stopped. About how many days would it take you to write the numbers from 1 to 1 000 000?

2. How many times as great as 1 million is 1 billion? Use that number and your answer to Problem 1. Find how long it would take for 1 billion seconds to pass.

3. The average house spider has a mass of 0.0001 kg. Suppose you wanted to collect 1 kg of these spiders. Estimate the number of spiders you would need.

4. One estimate of Earth's age is 15 billion years. Fossils date the dinosaur Stegosaurus at about 150 million years. According to these estimates, about how many times as old as the dinosaur fossil is Earth?

5. *My Journal:* How does 1 billion compare in size to 1 million?

Practíse Your Skills

1. Write each number as a power of 10.
   a. 10 000
   b. 100 000
   c. 10 000 000
   d. 1 000 000
   e. 100 000 000
   f. 1 000 000 000

2. Write each power of 10 as a number.
   a. 10^5
   b. 10^8
   c. 10^{10}
   d. 10^7
   e. 10^4
   f. 10^2

FAST

What are the fastest and slowest animals, machines, or events that you know? How fast are you? Where do humans fit into the range of speeds shown on page 49?

1 How many times as fast as the speed of the planet Mercury in orbit is the speed of light? Explain how you solved this problem.

2 How are these speeds related: a penguin swimming, a river current, and a tortoise walking?

3 Pick five items from the chart on page 49. Make a graph to show the speeds. Explain why you chose the method that you did. Describe any problems you encountered, and how you solved them.

APPROXIMATE SPEEDS

Organism or Event	Speed in km/h
light	1 080 000 000
planet Mercury in orbit	200 000
planet Earth in orbit	107 244
Apollo 10 command module	39 666
rocket-powered airplane	7000
speed of sound	1218
tsunami	784
hurricane	200
spiny-tailed swift	170
skate boarder	125
cheetah	100
sailfish	96
killer whale	55
horsefly	38
penguin swimming	27
river current	3
tortoise	0.2
snail	0.005
glacier flow	0.000 5
bamboo growth	0.000 04
ocean floor splitting	0.000 000 08

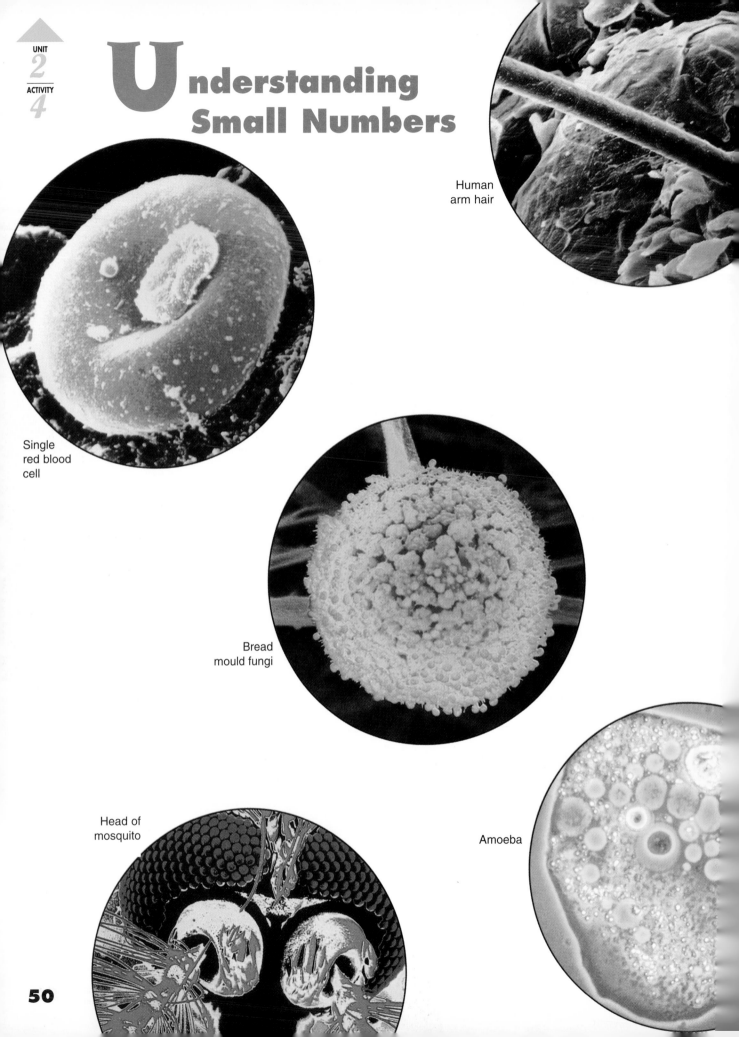

Understanding Small Numbers

Human
arm hair

Single
red blood
cell

Bread
mould fungi

Head of
mosquito

Amoeba

A micron is a unit often used to measure microscopic objects. One micron is $\frac{1}{1000}$, or 0.001 mm.

1000 microns = 1 mm

1. An amoeba measures about 0.6 mm in diameter. What is the diameter of an amoeba in microns?

2. Use an estimate of the diameter of one human hair in millimetres. What is the diameter of one human hair in microns?

3. Another common organism, often considered to have only one cell, is the paramecium. A paramecium may be about 125 microns in length. How many times as long as a paramecium is a 0.6-mm amoeba?

4. A human red blood cell is 0.007 mm in diameter. What is the diameter in microns?

5. *My Journal:* How is working with small numbers similar to working with large numbers? How is it different?

Practise Your Skills

1. Copy and complete. Write >, <, or = for each ■.
   a. 43.6 ■ 3.060
   b. 19.7 ■ 19.09
   c. 98.65 ■ 98.650
   d. 761.925 ■ 761.978

2. List each set of numbers from least to greatest.
   a. 0.385, 0.835, 0.358
   b. 6.802, 6.082, 6.82, 6.8
   c. 0.42, 0.245, 0.40
   d. 8.780, 7.80, 78.008

Metric Lengths

▶ Record data about several objects in a chart like this one.

Object to be Measured	Estimate of Length	Measurement of Length	Difference of Estimate and Measurement
1.	__?__ m __?__ cm __?__ mm	__?__ m __?__ cm __?__ mm	__?__ m __?__ cm __?__ mm
2.	__?__ m __?__ cm __?__ mm	__?__ m __?__ cm __?__ mm	__?__ m __?__ cm __?__ mm

1. How thick is a quarter? Would a stack of quarters 1 m high be worth more than $50? more than $200? Explain.

2. Would you write the circumference of a quarter in metres, centimetres, or millimetres? Explain.

3. Find the time it takes you to walk 10 m. How could you use the result of your walk to estimate the time you would take to walk 1 km?

4. One decimetre is 10 cm. Name two objects that are about 1 dm long. Measure any object in millimetres. Write its length in centimetres, decimetres, and metres.

5. *My Journal:* Describe how you can convert a metric measurement to other metric measurements. Give examples.

Practise Your Skills

Copy and complete.

1. 8 cm = ■ mm   2. 40 mm = ■ cm   3. 3 m = ■ cm

4. 750 cm = ■ m   5. 2.4 cm = ■ mm   6. 0.5 m = ■ mm

7. 7 dm = ■ cm   8. 500 mm = ■ dm   9. 4 km = ■ m

10. 247 m = ■ km   11. 0.4 km = ■ m   12. 5.6 km = ■ m

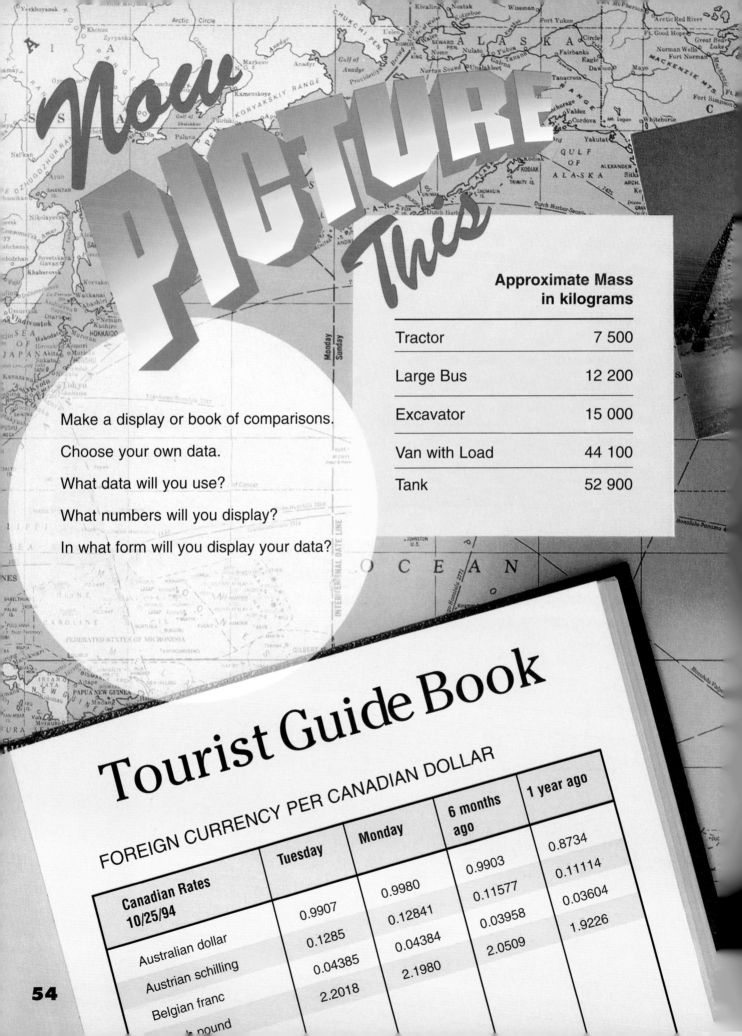

Now PICTURE This

Make a display or book of comparisons.

Choose your own data.

What data will you use?

What numbers will you display?

In what form will you display your data?

Approximate Mass in kilograms	
Tractor	7 500
Large Bus	12 200
Excavator	15 000
Van with Load	44 100
Tank	52 900

Tourist Guide Book

FOREIGN CURRENCY PER CANADIAN DOLLAR

	Tuesday	Monday	6 months ago	1 year ago
Canadian Rates 10/25/94			0.9903	0.8734
	0.9907	0.9980	0.11577	0.11114
Australian dollar	0.1285	0.12841	0.03958	0.03604
Austrian schilling	0.04385	0.04384	2.0509	1.9226
Belgian franc	2.2018	2.1980		
pound				

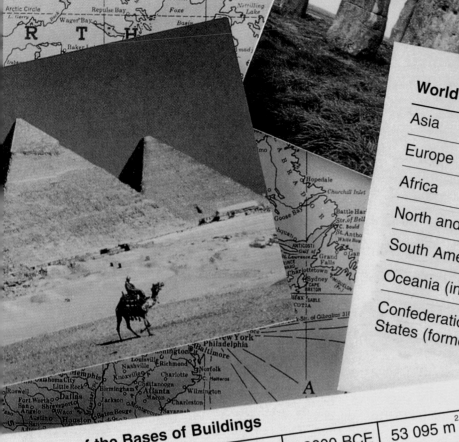

World Population Estimates 1992

Asia	
Europe	3 235 000 000
Africa	504 055 000
North and Central America	681 700 000
South America	435 600 000
Oceania (including Australia)	304 500 000
Confederation of Independent States (formerly U.S.S.R.)	27 500 000
	293 000 000

United Nations, 1992

Areas of the Bases of Buildings

1	Pyramid of Cheops	Egypt	c.2600 BCE	53 095 m^2
2	Stonehenge	England	c.1500 BCE	819 m^2
3	Colosseum	Italy	70–224	23 225 m^2
4	Chartres Cathedral	France	1194–1514	5 574 m^2
5	St. Peter's Basilica	Vatican	1506–1626	36 446 m^2
6	Taj Mahal	India	1636–53	9 101 m^2
7	Pentagon	U.S.A.	1941–43	117 355 m^2
8	C.N. Tower	Canada	1973–76	17 187 m^2

Check YOURSELF

Great Job! You chose your data and numbers carefully. Your numbers were correct, and correctly displayed in an appropriate form of your choice. You described in writing how and why you made your display the way you did.

EXPLORING LARGE AND SMALL NUMBERS

PROBLEM BANK

1. Imagine you were given one penny on Day 1, double that on Day 2, then double that on Day 3, and so on.

   a. On which day would you receive about 1000 pennies?

   b. On which day would you receive about 100 000 pennies?

   c. On which day would you receive about 1 000 000 pennies?

   d. On which day would you receive about 1 000 000 000 pennies?

   e. Explain how you got each answer, a–d.

Day	Number of Pennies
1	1
2	2
3	4
4	8
5	16
6	32
•	•
•	•
•	•

2. Display these data in a chart. Order the data in some way. Write the numbers in standard form.

World Population Closing in on 5.8 billion!

Canada Has Highest North American Population Growth Rate — Population Reaches 29 Million

United States Population Now over 250 Million

Mexico's Population Surpasses 90-Million Mark

3. The distance around Earth at the equator is about 40 000 km.

   a. About how many times would you need to travel around Earth to travel 1 million kilometres?

   b. About how many times would you need to travel around Earth to travel 1 billion kilometres?

4. The Patu marplesi is the smallest known spider. It is 0.43 mm long. About how many of these spiders could fit from the tip of your middle finger to the base of your hand? Explain how you decided.

5. The largest butterfly has a wing span of 280 mm. The smallest butterfly's wing span is 2 mm. About how many times as great as the smallest butterfly's wing span is the largest butterfly's wing span? Draw a diagram to show the difference in these measures.

The Queen Alexandra's birdwing butterfly – 280 mm wing span

6. Choose several objects in the room. Estimate their lengths. Measure them and record the measurements. Use a chart like this:

Object to be Measured	Estimate of Length	Measurement of Length	Difference of Estimate and Measurement

7. Use the measures of the objects in Problem 6. Write them in as many different units of measure as you can.

1. List the numbers in each set from least to greatest.

   a. 76 081 887   **b.** 97 818 214   **c.** 3 467 285

         102 901 106   9 781 921   630 275

          97 000 000   91 919 214   23 410 000

2. Copy and complete. Write > or < for each ■.

   a. 635 280 ■ 90 627

   b. 266 529 381 ■ 266 529 904

   c. 740 002 123 ■ 99 056 370

   d. 1 000 000 ■ 999 964

3. Round each number to the nearest whole number.

   a. 1728.450   **b.** 85.502   **c.** 2859.099   **d.** 0.682

4. Round each number to the nearest tenth, then hundredth.

   a. 8.715   **b.** 5.905   **c.** 12.007

   d. 68.555   **e.** 0.073   **f.** 16.938

5. Write each number as a power of 10.

   a. 100   **b.** 10 000   **c.** 1 000 000   **d.** 1000

6. Write each power of 10 as a number.

   a. 10^3 **b.** 10^6 **c.** 10^9 **d.** 10^{10}

7. Copy and complete.

   a. 0.17 m = ■ cm   **b.** 6 dm = ■ cm   **c.** 0.75 m = ■ mm

   d. 360 mm = ■ cm   **e.** 540 mm = ■ dm   **f.** 5.7 km = ■ m

1. Here is a T-table showing baby-sitting earnings.

Hours	Earnings ($)
1	3
2	6
3	9
4	12

   a. How much will be earned in 8 hours?

   b. Graph the data.

2. Make a T-table using the rule "multiply by 3, subtract 3."

3. What rule relates the first two columns to the third?

   a. 9   7   2   **b.** 1   4   6
       2   1   1   2   1   5
       5   2   3   3   2   8
       8   6   2   4   3   11

4. Write each number in standard form.

   a. 23 million   **b.** 2.5 million   **c.** 6 billion

5. **a.** Round 248 172 to the nearest thousand.

   b. Round 65.48 to the nearest tenth.

   c. Round 7.315 to the nearest hundredth.

6. Write each number as a power of 10.

   a. 10   **b.** 100 000   **c.** 10 000 000

7. Copy and complete.

   a. 6 cm = ■ mm   **b.** 0.5 m = ■ cm   **c.** 22 mm = ■ cm

   d. 120 cm = ■ m   **e.** 1.5 km = ■ m   **f.** 3000 m = ■ km

8. List each set of numbers from least to greatest.

   a. 4.207   4.072   7.42   2.704

   b. 5.3   5.31   5.033   5.133

SALE

Super Balls
2 for $3.00

and

Stop Watch
$9.99

ONLY $4.99

BLANK CASSETTES
BUY FIVE
GET ONE FREE

Super **SALE**

Nature Wear

We have a new line of clothing especially for the adventurer. Our designs are very comfortable and the quality is superb.

A. Team shirt $11.99

B. Sweatshirt $18.00

C. Hiking shorts $15.69

D. Baseball cap 7 colors $7.99

A.

B.

C.

D.

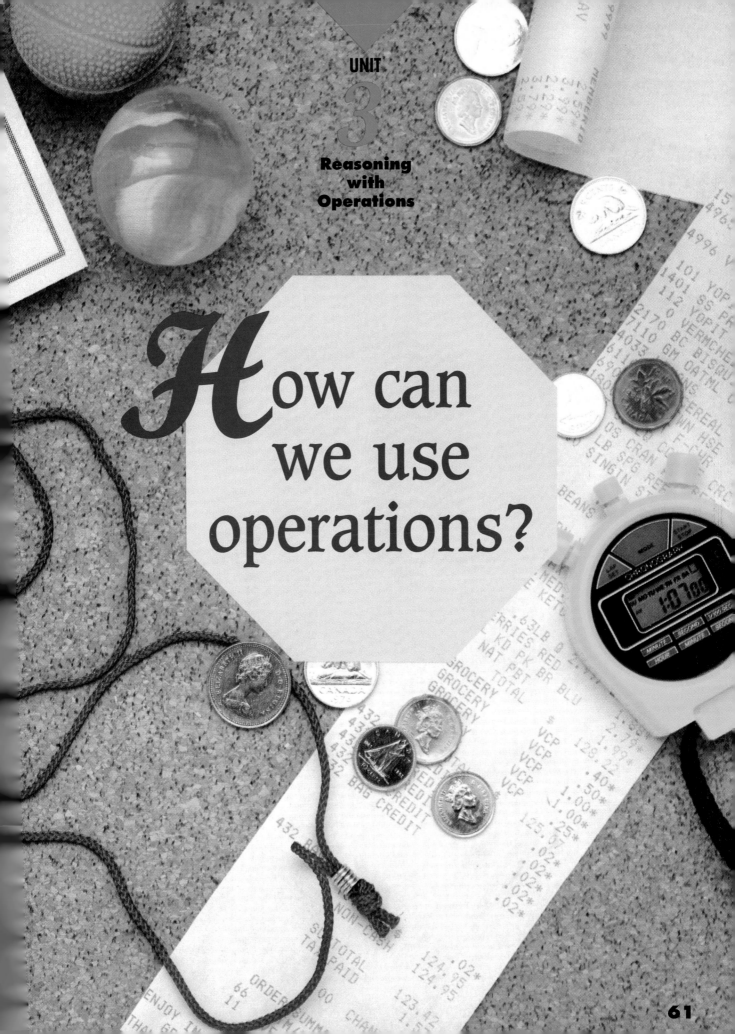

*H*ow can we use operations?

S·T·A·R·T·I·N·G OUT

SANDWICHES

Turkey	$3.75
Cheese	$2.50
Ham	$2.75
Ham & Cheese	$3.00
Tuna	$3.75
Chicken Salad	$3.50
Egg Salad	$3.00

SALADS

Chef Salad	$3.75
Spinach Salad	$4.25
Greek Salad	$4.25

HOT FOOD

Hamburger	$3.00
Hot Dog	$1.50
Beef Patty	$1.50
Vegetable Samosa	$1.00
Pasta of the Day	$4.00

French Fries	$1.25
with Gravy	$1.75
Grilled Cheese	$2.50
Soup of the Day	$1.50

DRINKS

Juice	$1.00
Milk	$1.10
Pop	$0.85
Coffee or Tea	$0.75

SPECIALS

Lasagna & Milk	$4.50
Soup & Sandwich of Your Choice	$4.00
Salad, Milk, Fresh Roll	$4.25

THREE SAMOSAS FOR THE PRICE OF TWO!
BUY TWO COOKIES, GET ONE FREE!
BUY ANY SANDWICH, GET A SECOND ONE A
HALF PRICE!

I'M DOWN TO MY LAST $5.00.

JUST GO PAID FOR B SITTING — GOT $6.

1 a. How can operations help each student decide what to have for lunch?

b. Are today's specials a good deal? How do you know?

c. How can operations help you figure out the best deals at the cafeteria?

d. What snack could you buy that would be both economical and good for you? How can operations help you decide?

My Journal: How can operations help you make decisions?

REASONING WITH
OPERATIONS

S·T·A·R·T·I·N·G

OUT

Brown Street School: Grade 6 Timetable

Time	Day 1	Day 2	Day 3	Day 4	Day 5	Day 6
8:45-9:05	OPENING EXERCISES					
9:05-9:45	Language Arts	Phys. Ed.	Language Arts	Language Arts	Phys. Ed.	French
9:45-10:25	Health	Math	French	Math	Math	Phys. Ed.
10:25-10:40	RECESS					
10:40-11:20	Math	French	Math	French	French	Math
11:20-12:00	Language Arts	Language Arts	Language Arts	Language Arts	Language Arts	Language Arts
12:00-1:15	LUNCH					
1:15-1:45	History	Buddies	Geography	History	Health	Art
1:45-2:15	History	Band	Geography	History	Band	Art
2:15-2:30	Recess	Band	Recess	Recess	Band	Recess
2:30-3:00	Science	Art	Science	Geography	Science	Language Arts
3:00-3:30	Science	Art	Science	Geography	Science	Language Arts

2 **a.** Suppose this was your timetable. Which would be your favourite day? Why?

   b. How can operations help you decide which day you like best?

   c. How can operations help you figure out a week in which you have your favourite subject most often?

   d. How is your timetable different from this one? How is it similar to this one?

My Journal: How are operations helpful in creating timetables?

Common Multiples

Jan and Peter practise figure skating at the same rink.
Jan practises every third day. Peter practises every fourth day.
They have agreed to practise together on the days that their
schedules coincide.

▶ How often will they practise together in 12 weeks?

Words to Know

Multiple:	the product of a given number and a whole number greater than 0; for example, some multiples of 6 are 6, 12, 18, and 24
Common Multiple:	a multiple shared by given numbers; for example, 12 is a multiple of 2 and a multiple of 3, so 12 is a common multiple of 2 and 3
Least Common Multiple:	the multiple that is the least among all the common multiples of given numbers

1. George takes a trip to England every two years. Manuel travels to England every three years. Jonathan visits England every four years. All three men took the trip in 1980. In which year will all three men visit England again?

2. Karen and Mark have part-time jobs at a restaurant. Mark works every 4th day. Karen works every 6th day. They worked together today. In how many days will Karen and Mark work together again?

3. *My Journal:* Describe how you would find the common multiples of two numbers.

Practise Your Skills

For each pair of numbers:
- Write the first 5 common multiples.
- Circle the least common multiple.

1. 5 and 8   **2.** 2 and 5

3. 4 and 9   **4.** 6 and 10

5. 6 and 8   **6.** 3 and 5

7. 2 and 8   **8.** 4 and 6

Exploring Factors

Mary has a 20-m by 30-m garden plot. This year
she decides to divide her garden into congruent squares.
Mary will plant different flowers in each square.
She wants to divide the garden so
there is no space remaining.

▶ In how many ways
can Mary
do this?

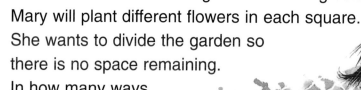

Words to Know	
Factors:	numbers used to form a product; for example, 3 and 5 are factors of 15
Common Factors:	factors shared by given products; for example, 3 is a factor of 12 and a factor of 15, so 3 is a common factor of 12 and 15
Greatest Common Factor:	the factor that is the greatest among all the common factors of given products
Prime Number:	a number whose only factors are 1 and itself
Composite Number:	a number with three or more factors; for example, since 9 has three factors, 1, 3, and 9, it is a composite number

Every composite number can be written as a product of at least two prime numbers.
For example, 21 = 3 x 7
and 12 = 2 x 2 x 3

To write 12 as a product of prime numbers, we first write 12 as a product of two factors.

4 is a composite number, so we write it as 2 x 2.
3 is a prime number, so we leave it as is.

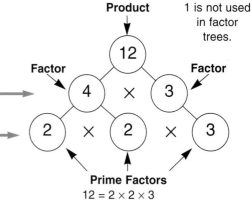

Note: The number 1 is not used in factor trees.

Prime Factors
12 = 2 × 2 × 3
This factor tree shows
12 as a product of prime factors.

1. Copy and complete each factor tree. Use the factor tree. Write each number as a product of prime factors.

a.
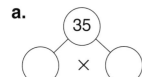

b.
22

c.
15

d.
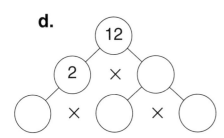

e.
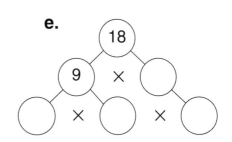

f.
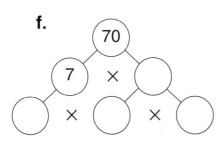

g.
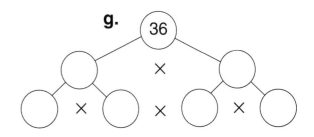

h.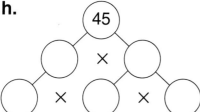

i.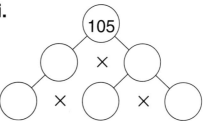

2. Draw a factor tree for each number. Write each number as a product of prime factors.

    a. 96   **b.** 100   **c.** 72

    d. 120   **e.** 200   **f.** 64

3. *My Journal:* Describe how you would make a factor tree to help you write 30 as the product of prime factors.

Practise Your Skills

1. Find the greatest common factor for each pair of numbers.

    a. 40 and 56   **b.** 24 and 40

    c. 16 and 32   **d.** 30 and 32

2. Copy these numbers. Beside each, write *prime* or *composite*.

    a. 57   **b.** 19   **c.** 91

    d. 100   **e.** 69   **f.** 12

    g. 37   **h.** 81   **i.** 46

A Calculating Machine

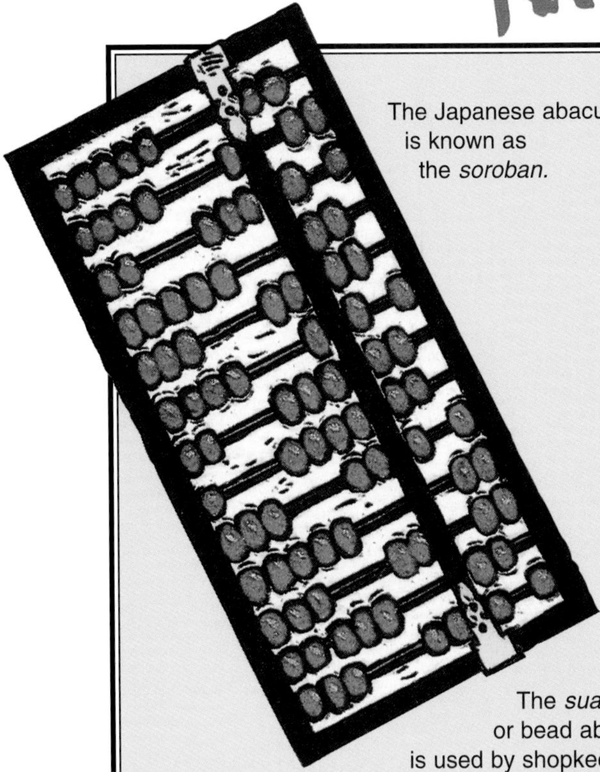

The Japanese abacus is known as the *soroban*.

Have you ever wondered how people in ancient times added, subtracted, multiplied, or divided? People in ancient Greece, Rome, Persia, China, or Japan may have used an abacus. On an abacus, people calculate by moving beads that represent certain numbers.

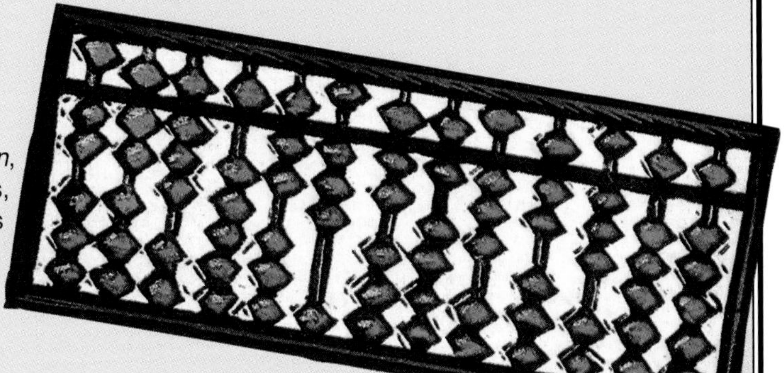

The *suan pan*, or bead abacus, is used by shopkeepers all over China.

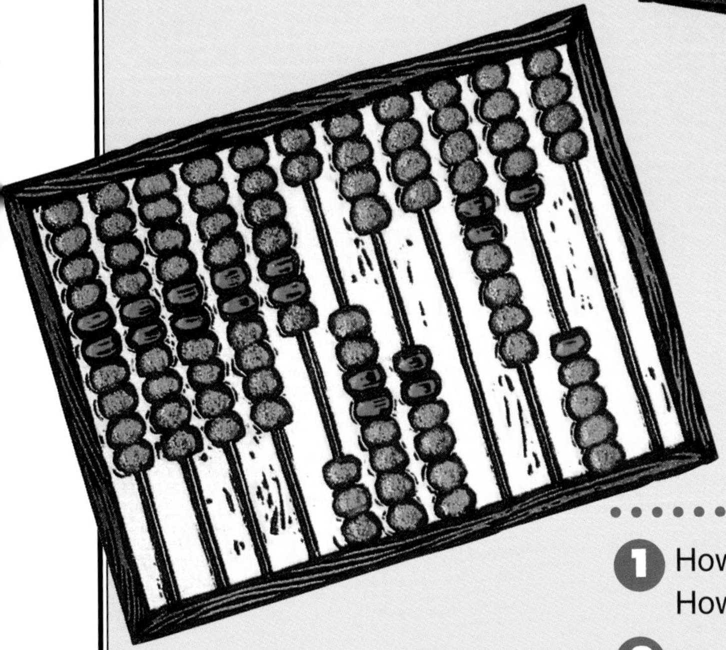

People who know how to use an abacus can add, subtract, multiply, and divide very quickly with it. Unlike a calculator, an abacus will never run out of batteries!

1 How are an abacus and a calculator different? How are they the same?

2 Choose an abacus shown here. Find out more about it.

S'choty is the Russian name for the abacus.

Exploring Addition and Subtraction

Aerodynamically engineered kite designed to fly in low or gusty winds. KK139 $18.95

The perfect sweat-shirt for the dog lover in your family. Specify sizes. S,M, L or XL SD548 $20.95

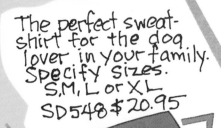

Touch tone phone. Keepin touch. LL803 $37.95

For members of the court, swift and stylish. GM017 $57.95

Listen to your favorite tunes even in the shower. SR599 $22.95

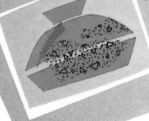

Microwave fast food, at home! CT118 $119.95

1000 pieces, the ultimate jigsaw puzzle! JP911 $14.95

JIG-PUZ-100 PIE

Warm and wonderful. FB014 $48.95

Look good in your brand new jeans! Even sizes 8-16 WB713 $19.95

You'll have no problem reading the outdoor temperature with this thermometer. OT886 $14.95

Set of four rice bowls adds cheer to any meal. CM476 $15.95

Keep all your CDs in one place. This tower in two sizes makes it easy to find the CD you're looking for. For 50 CDs CT501 $24.95 For 90 CDs CT901 $34.95

Fluffy absorbent robe, just ideal for stepping out of the shower. Child's S,M,L RC115 $29.95

Women's S,M,L RW116 $59.95

Men's S,M,L RM117 $69.95

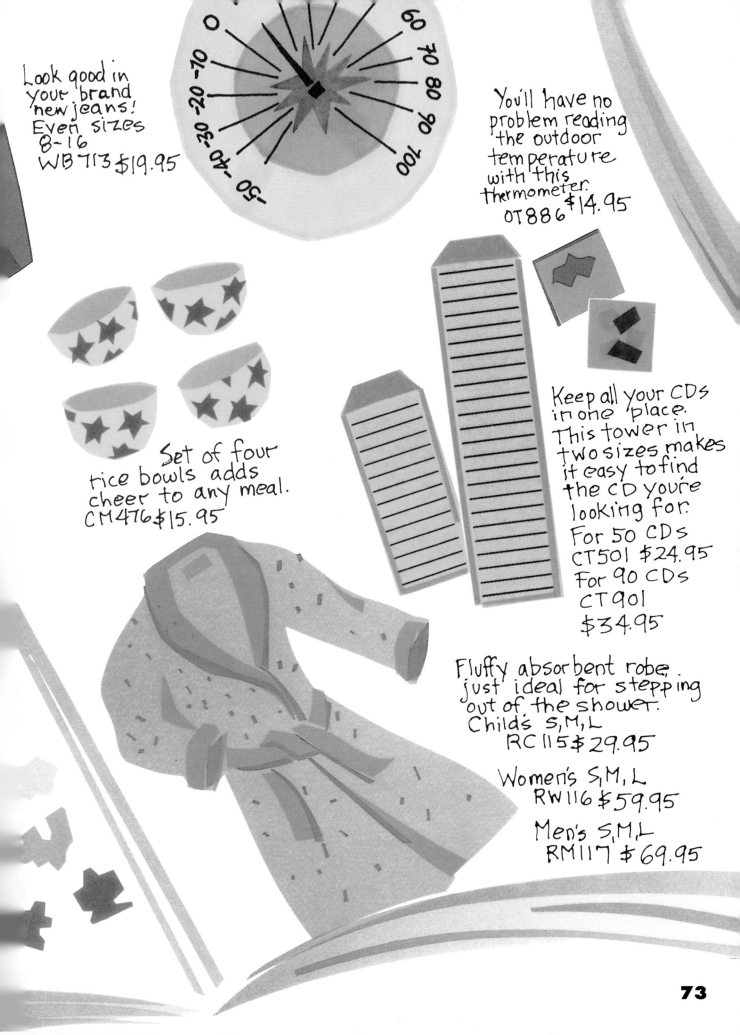

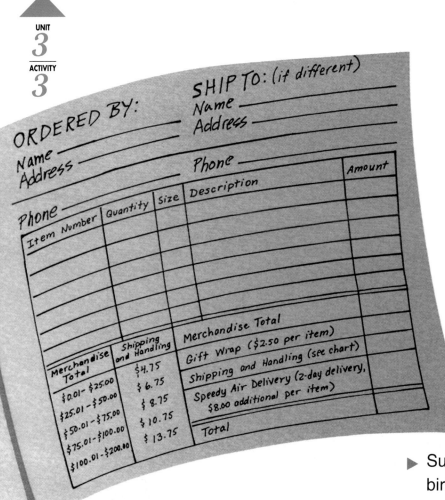

▶ Imagine you won $250. Suppose you want to buy six presents for members of your family or friends. You want the presents gift wrapped and sent by Speedy Air Delivery. What will you buy? How much will you spend in all?

▶ Suppose you got $75 for your birthday. What can you buy? How much will you have left?

Use the catalogue on pages 72 and 73.

1. Suppose you want to buy the shower radio. A friend told you that a nearby store has the same radio for $27.50. Would you order the radio from the catalogue or buy it at the store?

2. Imagine you have won the opportunity to go on a mail order shopping spree to buy presents for your family and friends. You may spend up to $150. What is the greatest number of items you can buy? What are the items? How much money would you have left?

3. Choose an item from the mail order catalogue that you would like to buy. Suppose you have $12.50. How much more money will you need to save to buy this item?

4. *My Journal:* How does estimation help in solving problems?

Strategies for Addition and Subtraction

▶ How did each student find 3.86 + 24.7?

▶ How did each student find 95.4 − 1.87?

Chalkboard Talk

$$\begin{array}{r} 24.70 \\ +\ 3.86 \\ \hline 1.56 \\ 27 \\ \hline 28.56 \end{array}$$

$$\begin{array}{r} 24 \\ +\ 3 \\ \hline 27 \end{array} \qquad \begin{array}{r} .70 \\ .86 \\ \hline 0.56 \end{array}$$

$$\begin{array}{r} 27 \\ \hline 28 \end{array} \longrightarrow 28.56$$

$$\begin{array}{r} 9\ 4\ 3\ 1 \\ 95.40 \\ -\ 1.87 \\ \hline 93.53 \end{array}$$

$$\begin{array}{r} 95.40 \\ 1.87 \end{array} \Big\rangle\ 0.13\ \text{to each}$$

$$\begin{array}{r} 95.53 \\ -\ 2.00 \\ \hline 93.53 \end{array}$$

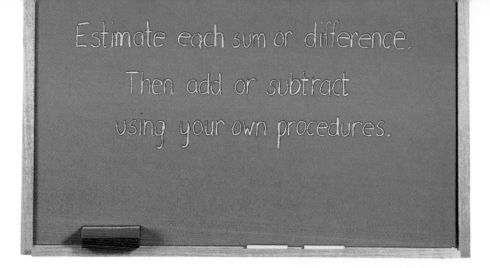

Estimate each sum or difference.
Then add or subtract
using your own procedures.

1. Make up an addition or subtraction expression. Find the sum or difference.

2. Find two numbers whose difference is 35.3.

3. Find four numbers whose sum is 147.65.

4. Rewrite the addition sentence 145.1 + 36.8 = 181.9 to give two subtraction sentences.

5. How do you check your work for addition?
   How do you check your work for subtraction?
   Give examples to show how you check addition and subtraction.

6. *My Journal:* How does estimating help when you are adding or subtracting?

Practise Your Skills

Add or subtract.
1. 327 + 52 + 4809 + 3   2. 5003 − 1998

3. 12.5 + 6.83 + 0.217   4. 3.6 − 2.804

5. 28 + 0.25 + 3.008   6. 75 − 0.927

Exploring Multiplication and Division

A 450-kg steer provides approximately 225 kg of edible meat. Of this, 20 kg are rib meat and 34 kg are steak.

The average person in Canada eats 23 kg of beef each year.

The average person in Canada eats 7.3 kg of hamburger buns or hot dog buns per year. There are usually 16 buns in a 1-kg package.

The most common items to put on a hamburger are 15 mL of ketchup, mayonnaise, or mustard, and 30 g of cheese.

Most beef comes from steers or heifers younger than three years old. They have masses between 315 kg and 495 kg.

**Life Expectancy
in Years**

Age in 1994	Male	Female
8	71	78
9	72	79
10	72	79
11	72	79
12	72	79
13	72	79

▶ Suppose all the edible meat from a steer, except rib meat and steaks, were ground into hamburger. How many 110-g burgers will a 450-kg steer provide?

▶ How many hamburgers and hot dogs would an average person your age in 1994 expect to eat in a lifetime? How many litres of ketchup, mayonnaise, or mustard would this person expect to eat on these hamburgers or hot dogs?

ON YOUR OWN

1. How many hamburger buns or hot dog buns can you lift? Explain.

2. How many 450-kg steers would be needed to feed your town or city for a year?

3. Here are the amounts of some popular food items eaten each year by the average person in Canada. Suppose your eating habits are average. How much of each would you expect to eat in your lifetime?

Peanut Butter
1.57 kg

Salsa
0.64 kg

Spaghetti
4.65 kg

4. *My Journal:* Do you think any one person will actually eat the amount of food you calculated in this activity? Why or why not?

Strategies for Multiplication

▶ Use a calculator. Determine where the decimal point should be placed in each product.

$$0.4 \times 0.7 = 28$$

$$2.32 \times 1.5 = 3480$$

$$0.05 \times 0.01 = 5$$

$$4.6 \times 0.29 = 1334$$

▶ What patterns do you see?
What rules can you write for determining the location of the decimal point in the product?

ON
YOUR
OWN

1. The product of 517 and 0.48 will be closest to which of the following numbers? Explain why you think so.

250   25   2500   25 000

517 x 048

2. The product of 300 and 0.91 will be closest to which of the following numbers? Explain why you think so.

2.75   27.5   275   2750

3. The product of 2537 and 0.13 will be closest to which of the following numbers? Explain why you think so.

3   300   30   3000

4. Find two numbers whose product is 3.48.

5. Find two numbers whose product is 0.45.

6. Copy and complete the table.

×	4173	0.54	13.7	0.03
10				
100				
1000				

7. Write to describe the patterns you see when multiplying a number by 10, 100, and 1000. Are the patterns different for whole numbers and decimals?

8. Copy and complete the table.

×	83	28	67	9
0.1				
0.01				
0.001				

9. Write to describe the patterns you see when multiplying a number by 0.1. 0.01, and 0.001.

10. *My Journal:* Describe how you find the number of decimal places in the product of a whole number and a decimal.

Practise Your Skills

Estimate each product. Then multiply using your own procedures.

1. 33.7×5 2. 4.8×52

3. 0.7×7 4. 48.2×23

5. 12.86×9 6. 72.06×7

7. 2.54×16 8. 53.5×19

Exploring Division

▶ Which store has the better prices?

$ $ $ FOOD MART $ $ $

2% Milk 4-L bag $2.99	Orange Juice 2 L $3.99	Tuna Fish 400 g $3.89
String Cheese $7.59/kg	Kidney Beans 796-mL can $1.89	Pita Bread 24-pack $1.99
Crispy Cereal 625-g box $4.75	Grape Jelly 500 mL $2.79	Rice 10-kg bag $10.49
Pierogis 350-g bag $1.29	Salmon $22.50/2 kg	Laundry Detergent 12 L box $7.99
Apples 2.27-kg bag $3.99	Peanut Butter 500 g $3.19	Toothpaste 100 mL $1.29
		Burritos 336-g pkg. $1.29

Dog Food 2-kg bag $4.59

Ketchup 1 L bottle $1.59

Ice Cream 1 L $3.29

Pretzels 1.36-kg bag $3.99

SAVE!

ON YOUR OWN

1. Look at grocery store ads for stores in your area. Which store has the best prices? How did you decide this?

2. Pick a food item at the grocery store or at home. Record several different brands and their sizes. Which is the best buy? How do you know?

3. Interview a member of your family who usually does the grocery shopping. At which store does your family usually do its grocery shopping? Why?

4. *My Journal:* In the future, how will you determine which store has the best prices? Why?

Grocery Land

SAVE!

Rice
2-kg bag
$2.99

2% Milk
1 L
$1.39

Kidney Beans
398-mL can
$0.69

String Cheese
224-g pkg.
$1.99

Grape Jelly
218 mL
$2.19

Laundry Detergent
8-L box
$5.99

Crispy Cereal
375-g box
$3.89

Salmon
$15.40/kg

Dog Food
8-kg bag
$15.79

Pierogis
500-g bag
$1.49

Peanut Butter
2-kg economy size
$8.59

Ketchup
375-mL bottle
$1.29

Apples
$2.84/kg

Tuna Fish
184 g
$2.19

Ice Cream
2 L
$4.99

Burritos
2-kg pkg.
$2.39

Pita Bread
12-pack
$1.99

Orange Juice
1 L
$2.19

Toothpaste
75 mL
$0.99

Pretzels
280-g bag
$1.99

SAVE!

Practise Your Skills

Estimate each quotient. Then divide, using your own procedures.

1. $9.64 ÷ 8 = $ ■   **2.** $17.69 ÷ 5 = $ ■

3. $25.99 ÷ 10 = $ ■   **4.** $1.98 ÷ 6 = $ ■

5. $27.3 ÷ 4 = $ ■   **6.** $0.65 ÷ 7 = $ ■

Strategies for Division

▶ Explain each procedure for finding 183 ÷ 12.

Chalkboard Talk

$$183 \div 12$$

```
        5
       10
  12 | 183
      120
       63
      -60
        3
```

$$183 \div 12$$

```
         15.25
   12 | 183.00
      - 12.
       -----
         63
        -60
       -----
         30
        -24
       -----
         60
        -60
       -----
          0
```

ON YOUR OWN

1. Find two numbers whose quotient is 21.

2. Find two numbers whose quotient is 7.5.

3. Will the quotient of 16 ÷ 64 be closest to 240, 24, 2.4, or 0.24? Explain your answer.

4. Will the quotient of 0.8 ÷ 5 be closest to 400, 40, 15, or 0.15? Explain your answer.

5. Will the quotient of 13 ÷ 15 be closest to 0.0086, 0.86, 86, or 860? Explain your answer.

6. Will the quotient of 18.2 ÷ 11 be closest to 1.65, 16.5, 165, or 1650? Explain your answer.

7. Copy and complete the table. Divide each number in the first row by each number in the first column.

	284	75	6	5.4
÷ 100				
÷ 10				
÷ 1				

8. *My Journal:* Describe the patterns you see in the table in problem 7.

Practise Your Skills

Divide using your own procedures. If necessary, write a decimal quotient. Do not show whole-number remainders.

1. 21 306 ÷ 50   2. 3 ÷ 8   3. 60.8 ÷ 19   4. 0.56 ÷ 3

5. 48 ÷ 24   6. 0.64 ÷ 8   7. 16.8 ÷ 12   8. 256.3 ÷ 18

Explain what you did with quotients that appear to continue forever.

Solving Problems Using Pre-Algebra Strategies

▶ Solve these puzzles.

1. I am a number.

Multiply me by 2.

Subtract 15 from the product.

You end with 21.

What number am I?

2. I am a number.

Add 25 to me.

Divide the sum by 2.

You end with 75.

What number am I?

3. I am a number.

Add me to 16.

Multiply the sum by 5.

Divide the product by 100.

The result is 1.

What number am I?

4. I am a number.

Add 4 times me to 25.

This sum is equal to 35

minus 2.

What number am I?

5. I am a number.

Double me.

Double that number.

Divide by 4.

What is the quotient?

AND THE NUMBER IS...

ON YOUR OWN

Solve each problem. Use any strategies you choose.

1. There are 13 cubes in a bag. Some are red. The rest are blue. There are 3 more red cubes than blue cubes. How many cubes of each colour are in the bag?

2. There are 8 kittens in a litter. They are black, white, or grey. There are 3 more black kittens than white kittens. There are 2 more grey kittens than white kittens. How many kittens are black? white? grey?

3. I am thinking of a number. If you subtract 14 from it, then multiply by 2, you get 32. What's the number?

4. *My Journal:* What strategies do you use to solve problems like the ones above?

Practise Your Skills

Use the clues. Find how many girls and how many boys are in each class.

Class Size	Clues	Number of Girls	Number of Boys
35	7 more boys than girls		
30	2 times as many girls as boys		
28	6 fewer boys than girls		

Solving Equations

▶ Find the unknown number in each equation.

1. $17 = \blacksquare + 5$

2. $7 \times \blacksquare = 84$

3. $13 = 21 - n$

4. $12 = t \div 12$

5. $7 + x = 8 + 9$

6. $25 - 9 = 2 \times \blacksquare$

7. $\blacksquare \times 6 = 84 \div 2$

8. $n + 2 = 30 - 4$

9. $d + 7 = 3 \times 7$

10. $48 \div b = 24 \div 4$

ON YOUR OWN

Suppose you have a balance scale and some 1-g, 5-g, and 10-g masses. What masses could you put in each empty pan to balance the scale? Solve each problem in at least two ways. Write an equation for each solution.

1.

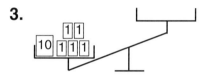

2.

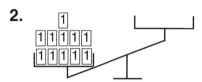

3.

4.

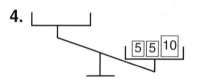

5. *My Journal:* What do you know about finding the unknown number in an equation?

Practise Your Skills

Find the unknown number.

1. $19 = n + 6$

2. $8 \times \blacksquare = 64$

3. $34 - 9 = 5 \times n$

4. $d + 7 = 40 \div 2$

5. $49 \div 7 = 14 \div \blacksquare$

6. $51 - 6 = n \times 5$

7. $16 = \blacksquare \div 2$

8. $12 \times n = 49 - 1$

Earning A COMPUTER

Determine whether your class could collect enough grocery receipts during the school year to earn a computer. If not, consider whether other classes in your school could work with you to accomplish this.

Write a letter to your principal, telling her or him whether your class or your school could do this. Explain how you made this decision.

COLLECT $190 000
in grocery store receipts!

GroceryLand

will purchase computer, monitor, keyboard, modem, and mouse for your school.

Offer ends June 1.

*C*heck**Y**OURSELF

Great job! Your letter explains clearly whether your class or your school could earn a computer. Your letter also explains how you determined this. Your letter shows an understanding of strategies for computation.
Your letter is clear and easy to follow.

PROBLEM BANK

1. For each pair of numbers, write the first 5 common multiples. Circle the least common multiple.
   a. 2 and 3   **b.** 6 and 9
   c. 4 and 5   **d.** 4 and 7

2. Find two numbers between 1 and 25 that each have exactly six factors. What are the common factors of these numbers? What is the greatest common factor?

3. List all the numbers from 1 to 25 that have only two factors each. What are these numbers called?

4. **a.** Your family wants a pasta dinner tonight. What is the least amount of money you could spend at the restaurant?
   b. The restaurant next door to this one sells its pizza with three toppings for $8.95. Delivery is free. At which restaurant would you get the better pizza deal?
   c. You have $8.50. Select an appetizer and a main course. What can you order?

MENU

•APPETIZERS•
Salad: $2.50
Soup: $1.95

•MAIN COURSE•
Pasta with meat sauce: $6.95
Pasta with tomato sauce: $5.95
Pasta with vegetables: $6.95
Pizza with cheese: $6.50
Pizza with 1 topping: $7.00
Pizza with 2 toppings: $7.25
Pizza with 3 toppings: $7.50

EAT IN OR TAKE OUT! DELIVERY CHARGE $2.00 PER ORDER.

5. Estimate the sum of 36 + 246.8 + 1.734. Then add using your own procedure.

6. Find two numbers whose difference is 135.82.

7. Rewrite the addition sentence 163.4 + 23.6 = 187 to give two subtraction sentences.

8. Estimate each product. Then multiply using your own procedures.
   a. 2.7 × 4   **b.** 3 × 4.1   **c.** 64.2 × 29

9. Find two numbers whose product is 7.96.

10. **a.** Would you rather get $400 a month allowance or $1 the first day, $2 the second day, $3 the third day, and so on?
    b. Would your answer to part a change, depending on the number of days in a particular month? Explain your thinking.

11. A music store is selling CDs for $17.38 each. The store has special offers of two CDs for $32.50 and three CDs for $45.98.
    a. How much are you saving on each CD if you buy 2? if you buy 3?
    b. How much are you saving in all if you buy 2 CDs at the special price? if you buy 3 CDs at the special price?
    c. Which is the best buy? Why?

REASONING WITH OPERATIONS

PROBLEM BANK

12. As part of Sean's science project, he has to calculate which brand of paper towel is the most economical.

	Brand X	Brand Y	Brand Z
Price per roll	$1.49	$1.19	$1.79
Number of sheets per roll	100	85	90

Estimate which brand is the best buy. Explain your thinking.

13. Natasha and Pia have decided to start a lawn mowing business. At the Chiu's house, they will be earning $15.00 a week for cutting the grass every Saturday in June, July, August, and September. At the Johnson's house, they will be earning $250.00 for the same job.

a. At which house are they earning more money? Explain your thinking.

b. Suppose the girls divide the money equally. How much will each one earn? How did you find out?

14. Find each mystery number.

a. I am a number.
Multiply me by 3.
Subtract 10.
The result is 5.
What number am I?

b. I am a number.
Double me.
Subtract that from 20.
The result is 4.
What number am I?

15. Write three equivalent expressions for the number 20.

16. Find the unknown number in each equation.

a. $21 = n - 9$ **b.** $64 = 4 \times s$ **c.** $19 = x + 7$

d. $30 = 90 \div k$ **e.** $15 - b = 9 + 3$ **f.** $15 + 10 = 5 \times t$

1. Write the least common multiple for each pair of numbers.
   a. 3 and 4   **b.** 5 and 7
   c. 6 and 8   **d.** 2 and 17

2. List the factors of each number.
   a. 54   **b.** 27   **c.** 40
   d. 18   **e.** 17   **f.** 36

3. Find the greatest common factor of each pair of numbers.
   a. 16 and 24   **b.** 12 and 32
   c. 24 and 30   **d.** 36 and 40

4. List 4 numbers that are prime. List 4 numbers that are composite.

5. Draw a factor tree for each number. Then write each number as a product of prime factors.
   a. 60   **b.** 78   **c.** 56

6. Add or subtract.
   a. $5672 - 2913$ **b.** $8047 + 391$ **c.** $632.5 + 27.38$
   d. $0.142 + 19$ **e.** $\$47.63 - \$1.94$ **f.** $1.921 - 0.03$

7. Multiply or divide.
   a. 986×30 **b.** 58.7×9 **c.** 268×8
   d. $859 \div 7$ **e.** $58.26 \div 3$ **f.** $2.5 \div 4$

8. Find the unknown number.
   a. $25 + n = 2 \times 18$ **b.** $42 - 9 = 25 + \blacksquare$ **c.** $18 \div 6 = \blacksquare \times 1$
   d. $51 = n - 10$ **e.** $n \times 4 = 15 + 9$ **f.** $b + 4 = 30 \div 2$

1. Write a rule for each T-table.

a.

Input	Output
8	4
9	5
10	6
11	7

b.

Input	Output
1	2
2	5
3	8
4	11

2. Plot these ordered pairs on a coordinate grid.
A(3, 4), B(2, 0), C(1, 5), D(0, 6)

3. Write the ordered pairs plotted on this grid.

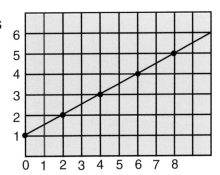

4. Copy and complete each expression with < or >.
   a. 6 097 428 ■ 14 985 023
   b. 23 842 000 000 ■ 9 843 973 000
   c. 8.47 ■ 7.842   **d.** 0.91 ■ 0.19   **e.** 2.054 ■ 2.405

5. Write each power of 10 as a number.
   a. 10^2 **b.** 10^6 **c.** 10^4 **d.** 10^8

6. a. Round 6 489 483 235 to the nearest million.
   b. Round 2841.565 to the nearest hundredth.
   c. Round 0.451 to the nearest tenth.

7. Copy and complete.
   a. 2500 m = ■ km   **b.** 3.2 m = ■ cm   **c.** 23 mm = ■ cm

2 BEDROOM FO...

Kitchen

Bedroom 2

Closet

Closet

Bedroom 1

Bathroom

Hallway

Office

Livingroom

72% Support Education ...ister's Decision

...nts and teachers in ...cton's Grade 12 ...s were pleased to ...that the recent ...ide math and sci-...sts written by the ...ned them scor-

...sult, the pro-...cation minis-...ided to have ...Grades 9 ...write similar ...ear to allow ...rents, and ...see how ...dents mea-

ank of Canada cuts bank rate to 6.45%

Reading Scores Up 2.6%

Students and teachers in New City's elemen-tary schools were pleased to hear that ...ding scores increased ...the last year.

Survey Shows 42% Want New Park

the possibilit... taxes to su... park, disag... park bour... concern w... traffic for... park. A t...

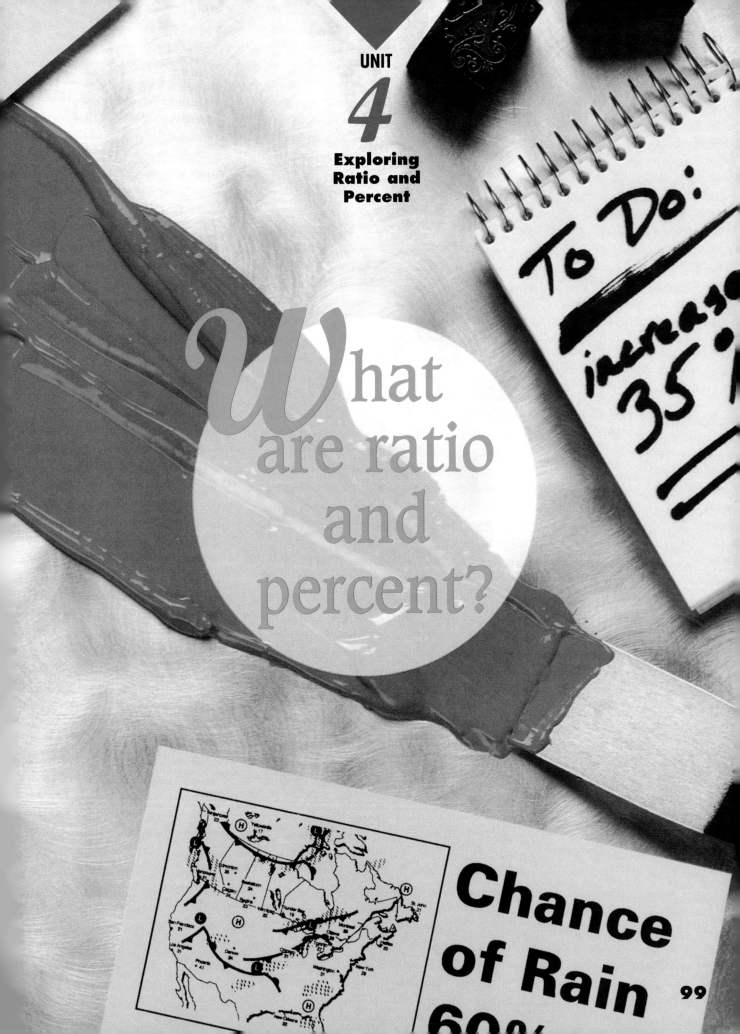

*W*hat are ratio and percent?

To Do:
increase 35

Chance of Rain 60%

99

EXPLORING RATIO AND PERCENT

30% off — what a great deal!

I hear there's a 50% chance of rain.

Yes! 90%! That's what I like to see!

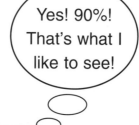

Sale 30% off

1 a. Everyone here is thinking percent. Rewrite what each person is thinking without using percent.

   b. At what other times have you heard percent being used?

My Journal: What questions do you have about percent?

Exploring Ratio

The ratio of boys to girls in Ms. Banerjee's class is 3 to 2.
How many boys might there be in the class?
How many girls might there be in the class?

Words to Know

Ratio: a comparison of two quantities; for example, ● ● ●

○ ○ ○ ○

The ratio of black circles to white circles is 3 to 4. This can also be written as 3 : 4, or $\frac{3}{4}$.

ON YOUR OWN

1. a. In the fruit punch, what is the ratio of orange juice to pineapple juice?

b. What is the ratio of juice to ginger ale?

c. What does each ratio describe?

6 : 3   2 to 3

5 : 11 $\frac{5}{6}$

FRUIT PUNCH

3L ORANGE JUICE

2L PINEAPPLE JUICE

6L GINGER ALE

2.

a. What is the ratio of green beans to kidney beans in the 3-bean salad? What is the ratio of kidney beans to lima beans?

b. What other ratios can you write to describe the salad?

c. How many cans of each bean would you need to make 8 bowls of salad? 12 bowls of salad?

3. *My Journal:* When might you use ratios in your daily life?

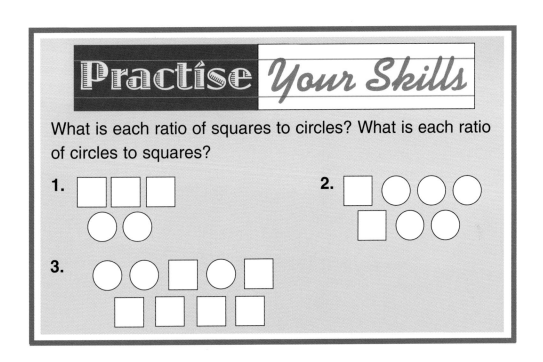

Practise Your Skills

What is each ratio of squares to circles? What is each ratio of circles to squares?

1.

2.

3.

Exploring Percents

Litre Sales	Unit Case Sales
1%	3%
(19)%	(18)%
27%	30%
16%	

major banks became a regular feature in most newspapers as the prime zig-zagged from a record high of 20% in April down to 10¾% in July and back up to a new all-time high of 21½% in Dec... The massive swi... in the

...ation in a ...
5%; ● Mai...

Average Annual Yield
Outperformed peer groups
22.2%
18.1%
17.5%
17.3%
S&P 400
S&P 500
Dow Jones Industrial Average

Chile 4%

Colombia 6%

Argentina 10%

Other 15%

Mexico 43%

Brazil 22%

MORTGAGE
6 1/4 % **6.** 65 % APR

...ks and Bonds

...e Stocks And B...
Up To 76%
If you...
Save

% Change
15.2
10.2
17.4
14.0
31.0
5.6
4.9
14.1

...ons great oppo...nities and challenges ...ecome a global company, and we are well along o... road. Five years ago, 13% of our sales were inter... tional. Since then, such sales have increased 174% which is an even more rapid pace of expansion tha...

he weather forecast shows 0% chance of rain tonight owed by clearing skies in morning."

20% DISCOUNT
EVERY ITEM ~ EVERY DAY
HOUSANDS IN STOC...
...ry made • Custom • Recove...
Mountings & Repai...
...s Experien...

...ns am...ous political and e... ...nation's u...
challenges at home. ▶ A land... ...ic re... about 90% complete... ...iet...
Talbott t...

% CHG
+ 12.5
+ 12.5
9.8
8.8
8.0
7.7
...

...ior banks became a regular feature ...host newspapers as the prime zig-...d from a record high of 20% in ...down to 10¾% in July and back ... new all-time high of 21½% in ...The massive swi... ...es were inter... ...d we are great opportunities and ... ...ecome a global company, and we are well alon... ...13% of ou...les were interna-... ...increased 174%, ... of expansion than our

...nvestmen... ...up 43.7%
...ons Fund ...ent survey... ...e workers... ...was a...
% OF
100
...Sound area

Average Annual Yield
Outperformed peer groups
22.2%
18.1%
17.5%
17.3%
S&P 400
S&P 500
Dow Jones In...

ALL TOYS 25%
ONE WEE...

ON YOUR OWN

▶ Use these three squares as benchmarks. Estimate what percent of each square is shaded in problems 1 to 4. Write each estimate using the percent symbol (%).

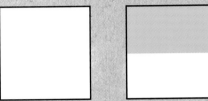

0% shaded   50% shaded   100% shaded

1. 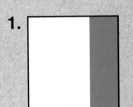 2. 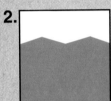 3.  4.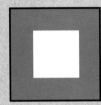

5. *My Journal:* Write what you know about percent.

Practise Your Skills

1. Draw a square. Shade about 50% of it.

2. Draw a circle. Shade about 25% of it.

3. Draw a square. Shade about 90% of it.

4. Draw a circle. Shade about 60% of it.

5. Draw a square. Shade about 10% of it.

105

The Meaning of Percent

▶ For the apartment, what percent of the total area is each room?

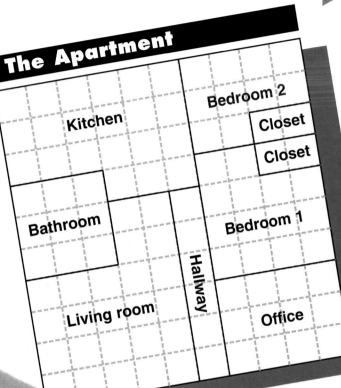

The Apartment

Kitchen
Bedroom 2
Closet
Closet
Bathroom
Hallway
Bedroom 1
Living room
Office

▶ Use a 10 by 10 grid. Draw a floor plan for the office below.

The Office Building

Room or Area	Number of Squares	Percent of Floor Space
Reception	12	12%
Copying and Storage	21	21%
Bathroom	6	6%
Office No. 1	30	30%
Office No. 2	20	20%
Hallway	11	11%

Tip

When you draw floor plans, label all the rooms and spaces you have created. Be sure to work in pencil; you may need to make changes to your plans.

▶ Use a 10 by 10 grid. Design a floor plan for this section of the school building. Then copy and complete the table.

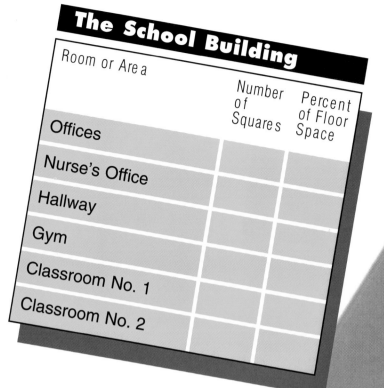

The School Building

Room or Area	Number of Squares	Percent of Floor Space
Offices		
Nurse's Office		
Hallway		
Gym		
Classroom No. 1		
Classroom No. 2		

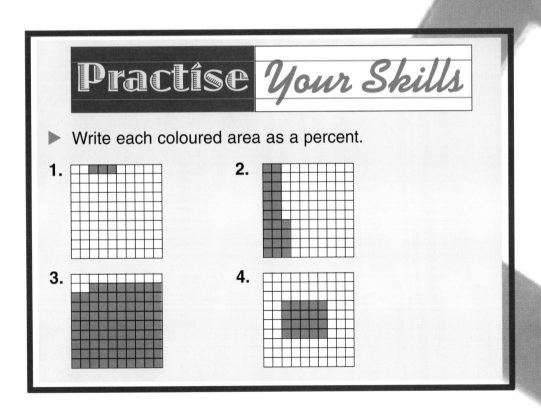

Practise Your Skills

▶ Write each coloured area as a percent.

1.

2.

3.

4.

Percent of the Whole

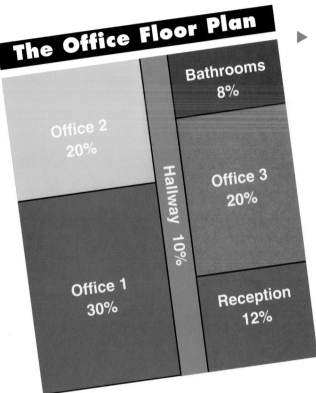

The Office Floor Plan

- Bathrooms 8%
- Office 2 20%
- Hallway 10%
- Office 3 20%
- Office 1 30%
- Reception 12%

▶ Describe the office floor plan.

The Apartment

Room or Area	Percent of Floor Space
Living room	35%
Kitchen	15%
Bedroom No. 1	18%
Bedroom No. 2	15%
Bathroom	10%
Closet	2%
Hallway	5%

▶ Use the information in the table for the apartment. Draw three different floor plans. Use apartments with these shapes.

▶ Copy the figures onto grid paper. Colour them as described.

1. Colour about 60% of the rectangle.

2. Colour the square to show four sections of 25% each.

3. Colour the rectangle to show 50%. Then use 3 other colours and 3 different percents to fill in the rest of the rectangle. Write the percent next to each colour.

4. *My Journal:* What do you know about percent and the size and shape of the whole?

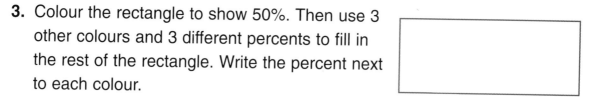

1. Write the area of each sector as a percent of the whole.

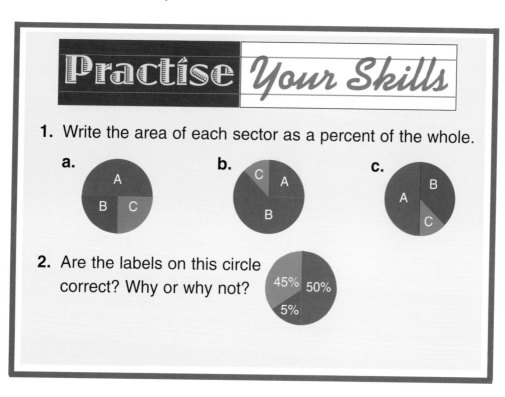

2. Are the labels on this circle correct? Why or why not?

45% 50%
5%

Percent Relative to the Whole

▶ For each line segment below, draw and label one that is about the same length. Then estimate to label points to show 25%, 50%, and 75% of each segment.

1 0%　　　　　　　　100%

2 0%　　　　　　　　　　　　　100%

3 0%　　　　　　　100%

▶ Copy each line segment. Label it to show 0% and 100%. Then label your estimates for 33% and 66% of each segment.

4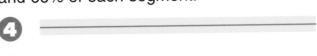

5

▶ Copy each line segment. Use the information shown to label the 100% point for each. Extend a line segment if necessary.

6 0%　　　　　　50%

7 0%　　　　75%

8 0%　25%

9 Suppose the people at the right are standing in a line for carnival tickets. The ticket seller estimates there are only enough tickets for 75% of them. About how many people will not get tickets?

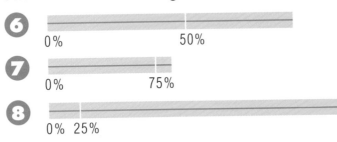

ON YOUR OWN

Sense or Nonsense?

▶ Tell whether each statement makes sense. For those that do not, write to explain why.

1. Martita said her height is 50% of Erin's height.

2. Pia read 137 pages of a 200-page book. She estimates she has read 45% of the book.

3. Ralph spent 100% of his allowance last week. Nico spent about half of his. Nico is sure he spent more money than Ralph did.

4. Irene told Bob she agreed with his plan 100%, except for his ideas about the estimated budget.

5. *My Journal:* What percents are difficult to estimate? Why? What percents are easy to estimate? Why?

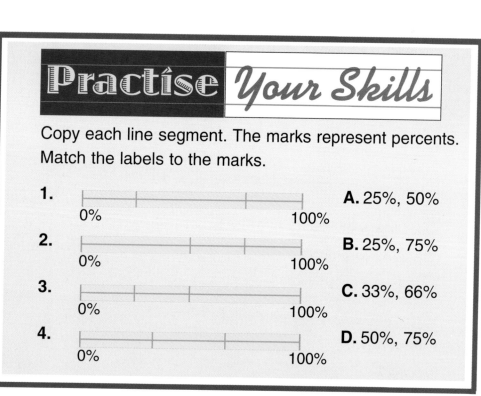

Practise Your Skills

Copy each line segment. The marks represent percents. Match the labels to the marks.

1. 0% 100% **A.** 25%, 50%

2. 0% 100% **B.** 25%, 75%

3. 0% 100% **C.** 33%, 66%

4. 0% 100% **D.** 50%, 75%

Healthy BY Percent

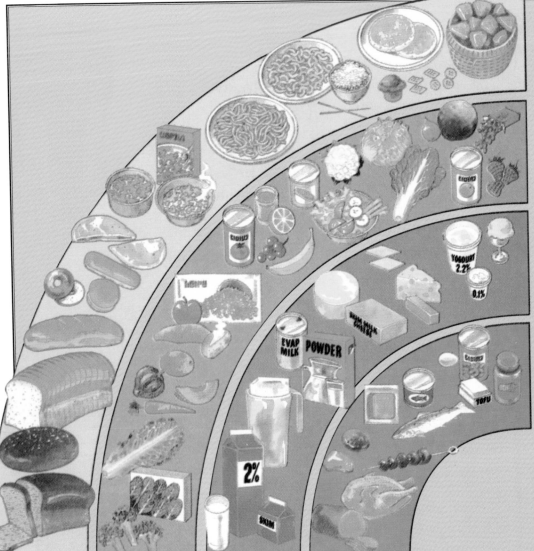

Grain Products
Choose whole grain and enriched products more often.

Vegetables & Fruit
Choose dark green and orange vegetables, and orange fruit more often.

Milk Products
Choose lower-fat milk products more often.

Meat & Alternatives
Choose leaner meats, poultry, and fish, as well as dried peas, beans, and lentils more often.

Have you ever wondered if your diet is as healthful as someone else's?

Here's a way to find out. Write down everything you eat for a day. Write what you eat and how much. Identify the food group in which each food belongs.

Do you have foods from each major food group? Look at the nutritional information on boxes, packages, in cook books, or in special books. Find out how many nutrients and calories you ate. Watch out for fats!

E xchange your data with a partner. Compare the healthfulness of your diets. Then select a meal with foods of different origins. Check the foods for nutrients and calories. Discuss and compare your information. How is the food you eat similar to the food you researched? How is it different? In which foods is there very little fat? Are any essential nutrients missing? Do you think you would like to try some of the foods you researched? What is important for a healthful diet, no matter which foods you're looking at?

In this game, you will make fractions less than 1. You will estimate the closest percent for each fraction.

THE CLOSEST PERCENT

Group
pair of students

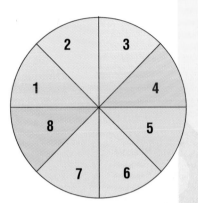

Materials
Paper clip (per pair)
Spinner divided into 8 parts and numbered as shown

Directions

1 Spin the spinner twice.

2 Use the two numbers. Make a fraction less than 1.

3 Estimate whether the fraction you made is closest to 0%, 25%, 50%, 75%, or 100%. Write to explain how you decided.

4 Make a chart. Record the fraction and the closest percent.

5 Include at least 10 fractions in your chart.

Fraction	Closest Percent (check one)				
	0%	25%	50%	75%	100%

Tip

Drawing a picture may help you estimate the percents.

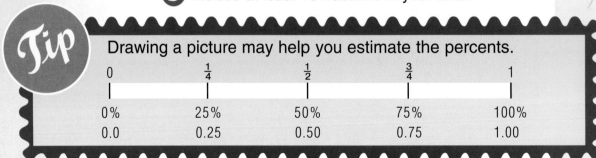

0	$\frac{1}{4}$	$\frac{1}{2}$	$\frac{3}{4}$	1
0%	25%	50%	75%	100%
0.0	0.25	0.50	0.75	1.00

ON YOUR OWN

▶ Tell whether each statement makes sense. For those that do not, write to explain.

1. Joachim ran 2 km in the 10-km race. He said he ran almost 50% of the way.

2. Karen saved $\frac{3}{4}$ of her allowance. She told her friends she spent only 25% of her allowance.

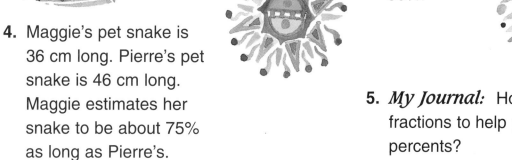

3. Zita bought a $90.00 pair of skates for $60.00. She said she saved about 30%.

4. Maggie's pet snake is 36 cm long. Pierre's pet snake is 46 cm long. Maggie estimates her snake to be about 75% as long as Pierre's.

5. *My Journal:* How can you use fractions to help you know percents?

Practise Your Skills

Tell whether each fraction is closest to 0%, 25%, 50%, 75%, or 100%.

1. $\frac{1}{10}$ 2. $\frac{3}{4}$ 3. $\frac{1}{5}$ 4. $\frac{9}{10}$

5. $\frac{3}{6}$ 6. $\frac{1}{3}$ 7. $\frac{7}{10}$ 8. $\frac{2}{3}$

★ ANALYZING A ★
NEWSPAPER

Choose a local newspaper. List categories for items in the paper. What percent of the paper is used for each category?

Category	Percent of the Newspaper
News Stories	
Ads	
Photos + Art	

Use the percent chart you made on page 116. How can you design an eight-page newspaper layout with the percents in the chart?

CheckYOURSELF

Great job! The layout you designed had approximately the same percent for each category, as the newspaper you looked at. You explained clearly in writing how percents were used in creating your layout.

PROBLEM BANK

1. What cubes are described by each ratio?

   a. 3 : 6
   b. 2 : 1
   c. 6 : 9
   d. 9 : 3

   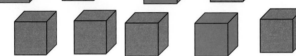

2. Use coloured tiles. Determine whether the ratios in each of parts
   a and b are equivalent.

   a. 5 : 2   10 : 4   20 : 8   **b.** 3 : 6   6 : 9   9 : 12

3. In which of these figures do you think about 50% is shaded?
   Explain your thinking. Draw 3 different shaped rectangles.
   For each rectangle, shade 50%.

   a.

   b.
   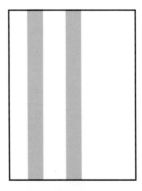

   c.

   d.
   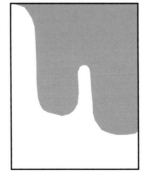

4. Here are some layouts for a class newspaper.

i.

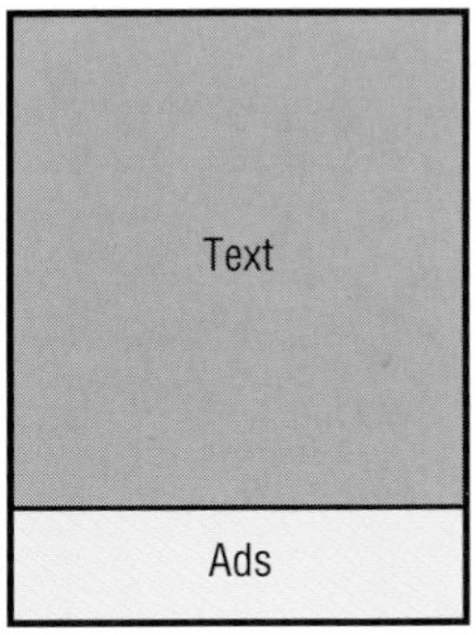

Text
Ads

ii.

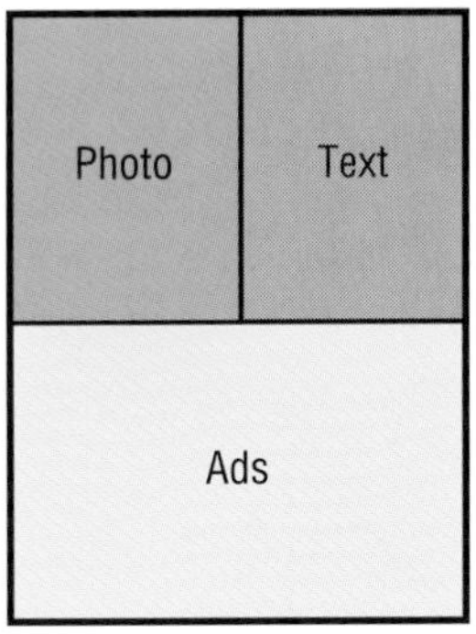

Photo	Text
Ads	

iii.

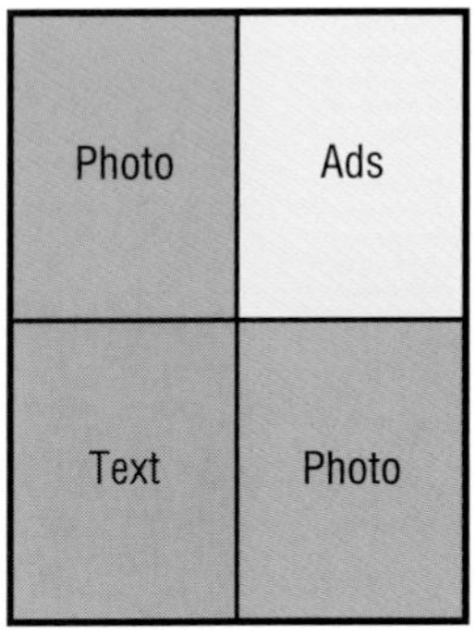

Photo	Ads
Text	Photo

iv.

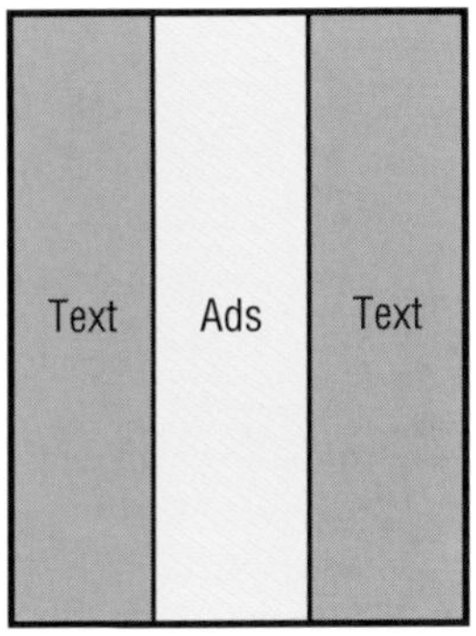

Text	Ads	Text

v.

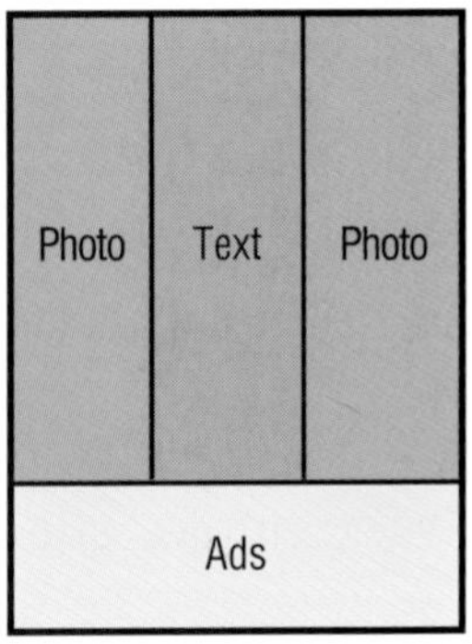

Photo	Text	Photo
Ads		

a. Which layouts do you think have about 50% photos?

b. Which layouts do you think have about 25% text?

c. Which layouts do you think have more than 75% text?

d. Which layouts do you think have about 25% text and 50% ads?

5. Use a 10 by 10 grid. Use 3 or 4 colours to create an interesting design on the grid. Write about your design. Use percent to tell about how much of the grid is each colour.

PROBLEM
BANK

6. Here are two floor plans for the new community centre. The designers were told:

- to include a gym, pool, dance studio, change room, and an art studio
- the gym should be the largest space
- the dance studio should be larger than the art studio
- not to use more than 15% of the space for hallways

Which plan do you think will be accepted? Explain your thinking.

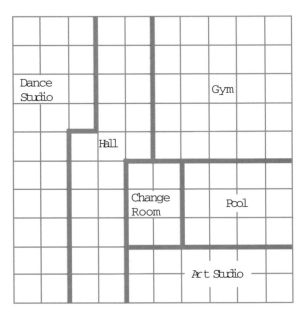

Plan A

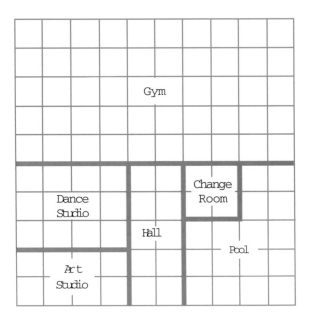

Plan B

7. A school received a block of free baseball tickets. There were only enough tickets for 25% of the students. There were 200 students in the school. About how many students received tickets for the game?

8. Here is a circle graph. It shows how students in a grade six class spend their time on a weekday. The label for each section is missing. Copy the graph. Label it with the activities you think belong. Include the percent of 24 hours you think is spent on each activity.

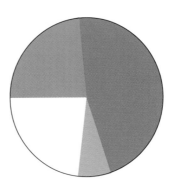

9. Here is a line segment. Draw and label one about the same length. Show the markings for 10%, 30%, 50%, 70%, 90%. Explain what you did.

0   100%

10. Tamra drew these lines. She showed why she thought 50% could sometimes be 75%. What would you tell Tamra to help her understand percent?

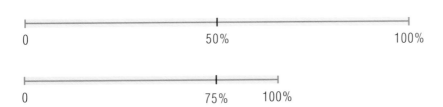

0   50%   100%

0   75%   100%

S K I L L BANK
FROM THIS UNIT

1. Name each ratio for the circles.
   a. red to blue
   b. blue to red
   c. blue to the total number
   of circles

2. What percent of each square is shaded?

   a.
   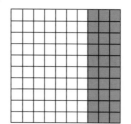

   b.
   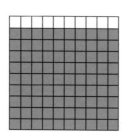

   c.
   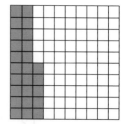

3. Draw three circles.
   a. Shade about 50% of one circle.
   b. Shade about 25% of the second circle.
   c. Shade about 33% of the third circle.

4. Draw a line segment 12 cm long.

0%   100%

On the line segment, label 25%, 50%, and 75%.

5. Match each percent to one of these fractions: $\frac{1}{3}$, $\frac{1}{4}$, $\frac{1}{2}$, $\frac{1}{5}$, $\frac{3}{4}$, $\frac{2}{3}$
   a. 50%   **b.** about 33%   **c.** 25%
   d. 20%   **e.** about 66%   **f.** 75%

S K I L L
BANK
LOOKING BACK

1. Write each number in standard form.
  a. 16 billion   **b.** 4.8 million   **c.** 67 hundredths

2. List the numbers in each set from least to greatest.
  a. 16.4   61.1   4.6   6.11   **b.** 0.2   0.08   0.7   0.312

3. Round each number to the nearest hundredth, then tenth.
  a. 4.175   **b.** 0.238   **c.** 16.513

4. Write each number as a power of 10.
  a. 100   **b.** 10 000   **c.** 1 000 000 000

5. Copy and complete.
  a. 67 mm = ■ cm   **b.** 4 dm = ■ cm   **c.** 1.5 m = ■ cm

6. Write the least common multiple for each pair of numbers.
  a. 2 and 3   **b.** 4 and 5   **c.** 2 and 9

7. Write the greatest common factor for each pair of numbers.
  a. 9 and 12   **b.** 15 and 20   **c.** 16 and 24

8. Add or subtract.
  a. 17.8 + 4.91   **b.** $387.14 − $39.50   **c.** 580.4 + 80.54
  d. 3872 − 109   **e.** $390.05 + $16.67   **f.** 93.81 − 14.5

9. Multiply or divide.
  a. 483 × 54   **b.** 59.5 × 6   **c.** 619 × 90
  d. 882 ÷ 7   **e.** 46.15 ÷ 5   **f.** 2088 ÷ 6

Rising Bank Fees

Average Fee Increase (1989-1993)

Percent Increase

13%
16%
19%
24%
29%

Depositing Bad Checks
Money Orders
Stop Payment Order
Bounced Checks
Covering Overdraft

Type of Service

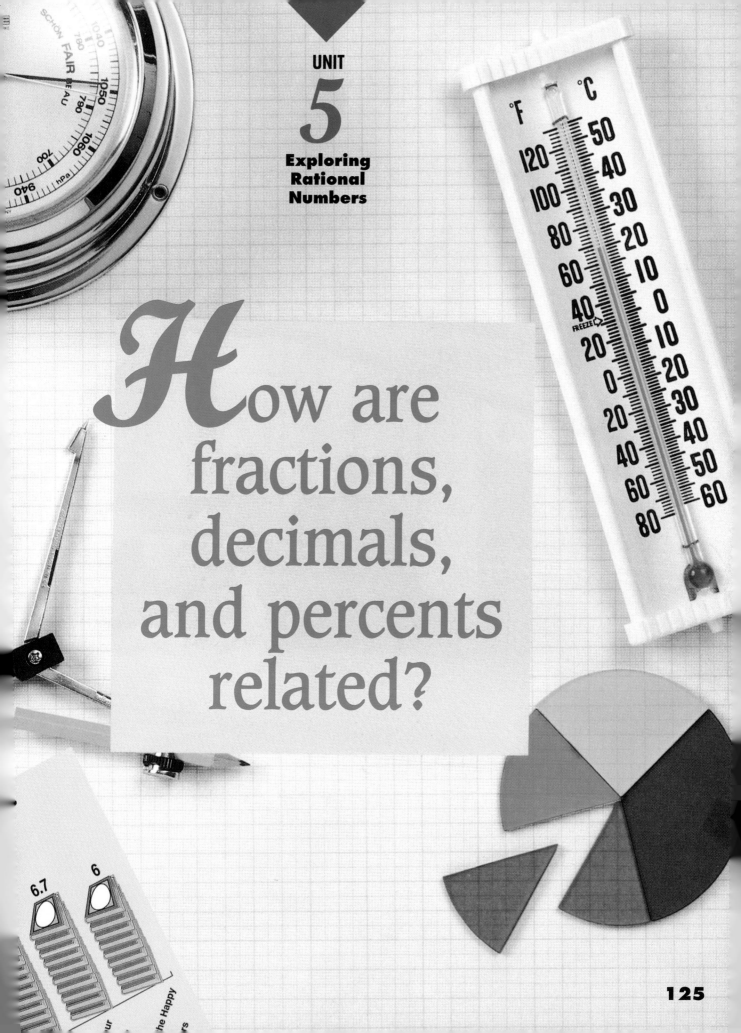

How are fractions, decimals, and percents related?

1 a. What things can you see that show parts of one whole?

b. What things can you describe using fractions? decimals? percents?

c. Where else have you seen fractions, decimals, and percents used? How were they used?

My Journal: What do you know about fractions, decimals, and percents? How do you think they are related?

**EXPLORING RATIONAL
NUMBERS**

S·TARTING·
OUT

JOHANNSEN

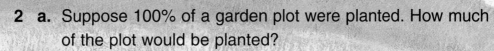

2 a. Suppose 100% of a garden plot were planted. How much of the plot would be planted?

b. Approximately what percent of each garden plot shown is planted?

c. How did you make your estimates?

d. In what other ways can you express the part of each garden plot that is planted?

e. How could you show that 60% and $\frac{3}{5}$ are equal?

My Journal: What questions do you have about fractions, decimals, and percents?

Using Ten-by-Ten Grids

The grid below represents one city block.

▶ What decimal and percent of the city block is represented by each of the following?

- $\frac{1}{2}$ of the grid
- $\frac{1}{4}$ of the grid
- ten small squares
- one small square
- the whole grid

▶ What number of squares on the grid shows each of the following?

- $\frac{3}{4}$ of the city block
- 15% of the city block
- 0.35 of the city block

Grid = 1 City Block

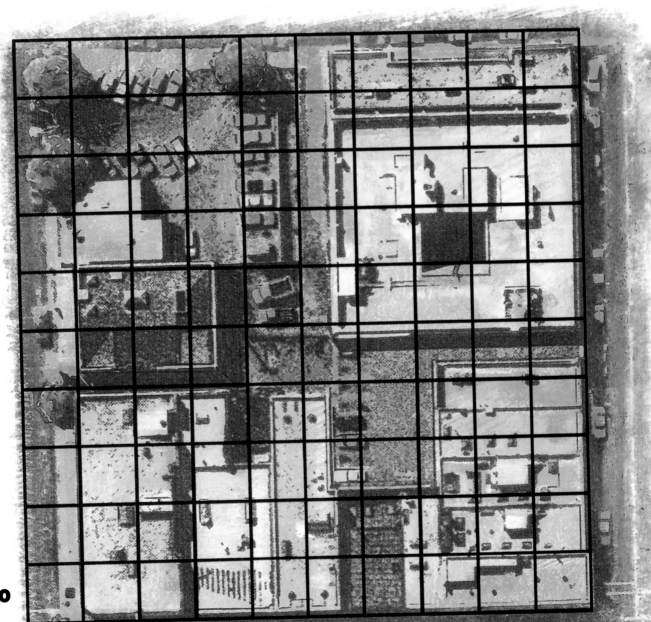

Each grid of 100 squares represents a different whole.

1   100 people

2   500 people

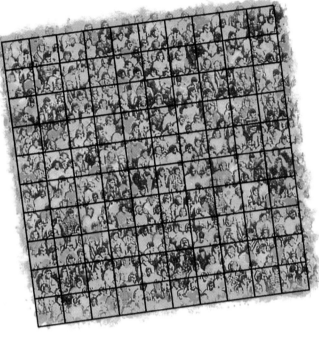

3   50 people

▶ For each grid, state the number of people represented by:
  a. 1 square, or 1% of the grid
  b. 10 squares, or 10% of the grid
  c. 20 squares, or 20% of the grid
  d. 0.01 of the grid
  e. $\frac{1}{5}$ of the grid

ON YOUR OWN

Solve these problems.
Use 10 by 10 grids if you wish.

1. A newspaper surveyed 200 students. Twenty percent said they have considered running for public office. What fraction was this? What decimal was this? Explain. How many of the students surveyed made this statement?

2. A school fund-raising drive plans to earn 80% of its goal by November 1. What fraction is this? What decimal is this?

3. At parents' night, the principal said only 40% of the students at John Jay School were involved in at least one sport. What decimal describes this part? Suppose John Jay has an enrollment of 600 students. How many students are involved in sports?

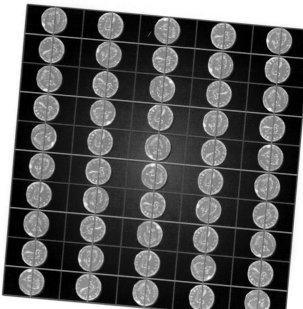

4. Suppose you received $50 as a gift. You are trying to save 30% of any money you receive for a school trip. What fraction of the amount you received is this? How much money should you save?

5. The school auditorium has 400 seats.

   a. Suppose the auditorium is 50% full. How many seats are filled?

   b. Suppose the auditorium is 70% full. How many seats are filled?

What fractions and decimals can you use to describe these percents?

6. Sid's cat spends approximately 75% of each day sleeping. What fraction of the day does this represent? About how many hours does she sleep in a day?

7. *My Journal:* How are fractions, decimals, and percents related?

Practise Your Skills

1. Express as a decimal.

   a. 50%   **b.** 20%   **c.** 80%   **d.** 75%

2. Express as a fraction.

   a. 25%   **b.** 40%   **c.** 60%   **d.** 10%

3. Express as a percent.

   a. $\frac{30}{100}$ **b.** $\frac{35}{100}$ **c.** $\frac{7}{10}$ **d.** $\frac{9}{10}$

   e. 0.65   **f.** 0.80   **g.** 0.2   **h.** 0.1

   i. $\frac{1}{4}$ **j.** $\frac{1}{5}$ **k.** $\frac{3}{4}$ **l.** $\frac{4}{5}$

4. Copy and complete.

   a. 0.61 = ■ %   **b.** $\frac{3}{4}$ = ■ %   **c.** 0.93 = ■ %

THE IN Between GAME

Group

Pairs

Materials

Each pair needs:
24 cards labelled: $\frac{1}{4}$, $\frac{1}{3}$, $\frac{1}{2}$, $\frac{3}{4}$, $\frac{1}{10}$, $\frac{7}{10}$, $\frac{2}{3}$, $\frac{9}{10}$, 0.1, 0.6, 0.5, 0.35, 0.75, 0.62, 0.87, 0.90, 10%, 16%, 25%, 50%, 45%, 80%, 75%, 90%

Game Rules

1 Shuffle all the cards. Each player gets three cards. Place the rest of the cards face down in a pile.

2 Each player turns over one card from the pile and places it beside the pile. These become the Target Numbers. The player who turns over the greater Target Number goes first. (Flip a coin if the Target Numbers are equivalent.)

Target Number $\boxed{\frac{1}{4}}$ $\boxed{90\%}$ Target Number

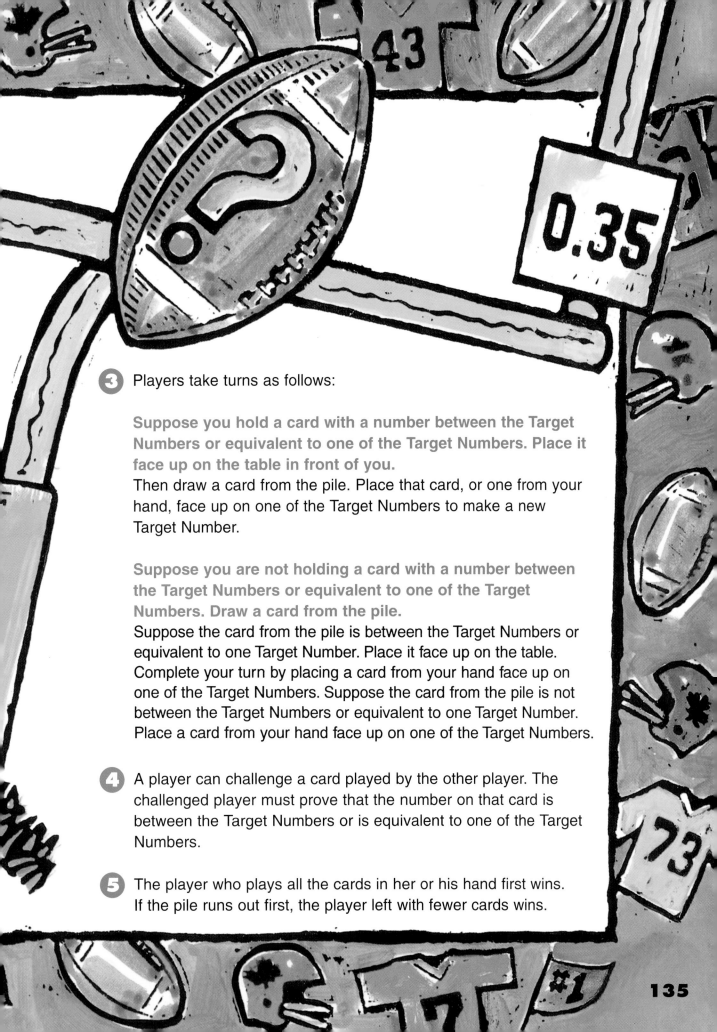

3 Players take turns as follows:

Suppose you hold a card with a number between the Target Numbers or equivalent to one of the Target Numbers. Place it face up on the table in front of you.
Then draw a card from the pile. Place that card, or one from your hand, face up on one of the Target Numbers to make a new Target Number.

Suppose you are not holding a card with a number between the Target Numbers or equivalent to one of the Target Numbers. Draw a card from the pile.
Suppose the card from the pile is between the Target Numbers or equivalent to one Target Number. Place it face up on the table. Complete your turn by placing a card from your hand face up on one of the Target Numbers. Suppose the card from the pile is not between the Target Numbers or equivalent to one Target Number. Place a card from your hand face up on one of the Target Numbers.

4 A player can challenge a card played by the other player. The challenged player must prove that the number on that card is between the Target Numbers or is equivalent to one of the Target Numbers.

5 The player who plays all the cards in her or his hand first wins. If the pile runs out first, the player left with fewer cards wins.

Exploring Integers

▷ What is the highest temperature on the chart? the lowest?

TEMPERATURE RANGES OF CANADIAN CITIES

City	April 24 high/low	April 25 high/low	April 26 high/low
Athabasca	7/-4	3/-9	1/-11
Calgary	9/-2	6/-5	3/-7
Charlottetown	9/0	11/2	12/0
Edmonton	7/-3	5/-6	3/-8
Fredericton	9/0	11/-1	14/1
Halifax	11/0	12/3	14/1
Inuvik	3/-9	2/-10	1/-9
Kamloops	16/4	15/2	16/3

City	April 24 high/low	April 25 high/low	April 26 high/low
London	21/6	17/2	18/6
Montreal	14/1	12/-1	17/3
Ottawa	12/1	14/-1	17/3
Penticton	16/4	16/3	17/3
Prince George	15/3	14/0	14/2
Quebec City	7/-2	9/1	12/5
Regina	9/-2	8/-8	3/-13
Saskatoon	7/-3	8/-6	9/-4

City	April 24 high/low	April 25 high/low	April 26 high/low
St. John's	8/-1	12/3	6/1
Sault Ste. Marie	18/7	14/6	15/3
Toronto	21/6	17/2	17/4
Vancouver	16/7	14/7	14/7
Victoria	14/6	14/6	16/6
Whitehorse	11/-2	9/-1	10/-1
Winnipeg	11/1	11/-2	9/-6
Yellowknife	4/-7	6/-6	0/-1

ON YOUR OWN

1. Find the high and low temperatures for your area for the next three days. Get your data from newspapers, the radio, or television. Record the data in a chart.

2. Use the chart from problem 1. Find and record the temperature difference for each day.

3. Use the data in your chart. Write a question you can answer. Answer the question.

4. *My Journal:* How are integers used to describe temperatures? In what other situations might negative numbers be used?

136

Absolutely the COLDEST

Did you ever wonder how scientists around the world represent temperatures?

Scientists around the world have agreed on many ways to represent data. They use the International System of Units, or SI, for all scientific measurement.

In SI, the Celsius scale is commonly used. However, scientists often use the Kelvin scale. It is named after the British scientist, Lord Kelvin.

Here's how the scales compare:

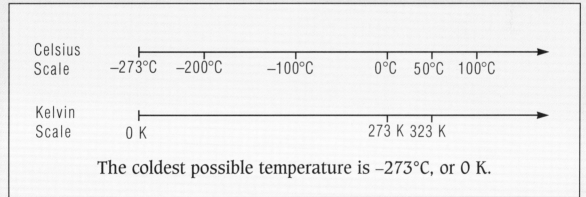

The coldest possible temperature is –273°C, or 0 K.

1 Are there any negative integers on the Kelvin scale? Explain.

2 How do the sizes of the units on each scale relate?

3 Why do you think scientists decided to use the Kelvin scale?

4 Which temperature scale do you use?

Exploring Integers

▶ Use the rating scale to tell how you feel about each statement.

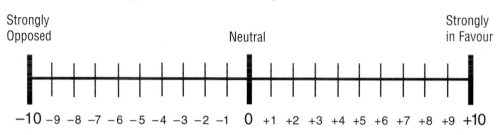

Strongly
Opposed   Neutral   Strongly
in Favour

−10 −9 −8 −7 −6 −5 −4 −3 −2 −1 0 +1 +2 +3 +4 +5 +6 +7 +8 +9 +10

1. Teenagers should not be allowed to drive until age 18.

2. Girls should be allowed to play football.

3. Students should do homework without music or television.

4. Students should be allowed to skateboard or roller blade in the halls at school.

5. All boys and girls should be required to take cooking classes.

6. Schools should be open 12 months a year.

7. School cafeterias should serve pizza and nachos every day.

Compare your ratings of the statements on page 138 with those of your partner. Then write at least six statements about your findings. Here are some things to consider:

- Who rated the first statement higher? How much higher is it?

- For which statement did you have the greatest disagreement? How much of a disagreement was it?

- Is there a statement that your partner rated higher than you did but to which you were both opposed? If so, how much higher did your partner rate that statement?

- Is there a statement that your partner was in favour of that you opposed? If so, how much lower was your rating?

▶ Draw scales or number lines. Show your ratings and your partner's ratings on three of the statements.

Use a number line or rating scale.

1. José rated his least favourite tape a –3. He rated his favourite tape 7 numbers higher. What was the rating for his favourite tape?

2. Angie rated her favourite movie star a +9. Her least favourite was 5 numbers lower. What was the rating for her least favourite movie star?

3. *My Journal:* What do you now know about comparing integers?

Practise Your Skills

Use a number line.
Which integer in each pair is greater? How much greater is it?

1. +5 or +9   2. −6 or −2   3. +8 or −4
4. −7 or +7   5. +3 or −9   6. −8 or 0

Creating a CLASS REPRESENTATIVE

How can you draw a proportional person who is representative of the students in your class?

1. Work with your group. Measure your height. Measure the length of each part of your body listed below. Write each length as a percent of your height.

   a. foot to knee   **b.** knee to waist

   c. waist to shoulders   **d.** shoulders to top of head

   e. shoulder to wrist   **f.** width of shoulders

2. Use these percents to find class means.

3. Work with your group. Use the class means to draw a proportional person who is representative of the students in your class.

charcoal
fusains

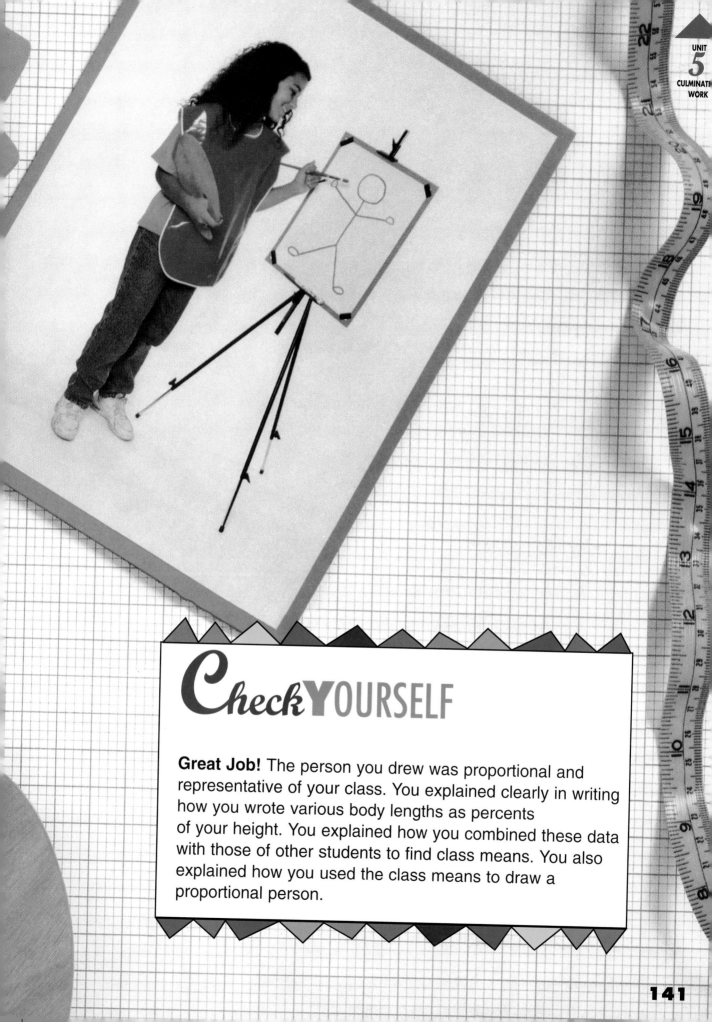

Check**Y**OURSELF

Great Job! The person you drew was proportional and representative of your class. You explained clearly in writing how you wrote various body lengths as percents of your height. You explained how you combined these data with those of other students to find class means. You also explained how you used the class means to draw a proportional person.

EXPLORING RATIONAL NUMBERS

PROBLEM BANK

1. Use a ten-by-ten grid. Explain to a friend how you know that $\frac{9}{10}$, 90%, and 0.9 are equivalent.

2. In a karate class there are 80 students. 25% of the students have earned a green belt.

   a. What fraction of students has earned a green belt?

   b. Express the fraction as a decimal.

   c. How many students have a green belt?

3. Approximately what fraction of each day do you spend sleeping? Express this fraction as a decimal and as a percent.

4. a. What percent of a dollar is each coin? a penny, a nickel, a dime, a quarter, a loonie

   b. Express each coin in part a as a fraction of a dollar.

5. Celine got 8 out of 10 problems correct on her first math test. She got 85% on the second test. On which test did Celine get the better score? Explain your thinking.

6. Look at each pair of test scores. Decide which is the better score. Write to explain your thinking.
   a. 8 out of 10, or 12 out of 20
   b. 75%, or 40 out of 50
   c. 89 out of 100, or 44 out of 50

7. Joe said he got $\frac{1}{4}$ off the price of a game he bought. Ari said he bought the same game at 40% off. Sara's discount was between Joe's and Ari's. What percent discount could Sara have had?

8. A school principal is doing the budget. If she reserves $\frac{1}{3}$ of the extra-curricular budget for sports, that is not enough for sports. If she uses 40% for sports, there is not enough money for other things. What percent of the budget could she reserve for sports?

9. In Vito's apartment building, the floor at street level is called the ground floor. There are 12 floors above the ground floor. There are 2 floors below the ground floor for parking. Draw a vertical line to represent the elevator in the building. Label it.

10. a. Write five or six statements on which you feel your family members or classmates would have opinions. Ask your family or some classmates to use the rating scale on page 138 to tell how they feel about each statement. Write to describe your findings.
    b. For each statement, find the two ratings that are farthest apart. Find the difference between them.

11. Maria used a scale of −10 to +10. She rated her favourite T.V. show +9 and her least favourite −2. Show her ratings on a number line.

12. Which rating expresses a greater degree of approval? Explain.
    a. −10 or −5   b. 0 or −2

1. Use a fraction, a decimal, and a percent. Describe the shaded part of each grid.

a. 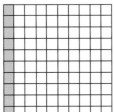 **b.** 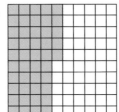 **c.**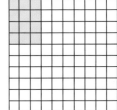

2. Write each fraction or decimal as a percent.

a. $\frac{39}{100}$ **b.** $\frac{7}{10}$ **c.** $\frac{6}{100}$ **d.** $\frac{1}{2}$

e. 0.18 **f.** 0.25 **g.** 0.06 **h.** 0.8

3. List each set in order from least to greatest.

a. $\frac{1}{2}$, 60%, 0.25 **b.** 38%, 0.62, $\frac{17}{100}$

c. 0.99, 40%, $\frac{4}{5}$ **d.** $\frac{3}{4}$, 0.20, 89%

4. Write an integer for each situation.

a. 2° below 0° **b.** 16° above 0°

c. $5 in debt **d.** $10 in savings

e. 3 floors above ground level **f.** 8 floors below ground level

5. Use the number line. Copy each expression.
Replace ■ with < or >.

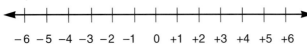

$$-6 \quad -5 \quad -4 \quad -3 \quad -2 \quad -1 \quad 0 \quad +1 \quad +2 \quad +3 \quad +4 \quad +5 \quad +6$$

a. +1 ■ +3 **b.** +4 ■ +3 **c.** 0 ■ +2

d. +1 ■ −1 **e.** −2 ■ +5 **f.** −3 ■ 0

g. −6 ■ −5 **h.** −2 ■ −4 **i.** −3 ■ +6

SKILL BANK
LOOKING BACK

1. List the factors of each number.
   a. 28   **b.** 24   **c.** 15   **d.** 50

2. List the numbers from 21 to 30. Beside each number, tell whether it is a prime number or a composite number.

3. Draw a factor tree for each number. Then write each number as a product of prime factors.
   a. 36   **b.** 70   **c.** 75

4. Calculate.
   a. $4832 + 607$ **b.** $3904 - 18$ **c.** $48.6 + 138.15$
   d. $19.3 - 0.12$ **e.** 437×6 **f.** 903×17
   g. 57.3×8 **h.** $3.48 \div 6$ **i.** $165.2 \div 7$

5. Find the unknown number.
   a. $32 = n + 8$ **b.** $20 - n = 16$ **c.** $n + 5 = 50 \div 2$

6. Name these ratios for the squares shown.
   a. blue to yellow
   b. yellow to red
   c. red to blue

7. **a.** Draw a square. Shade about 25% of it.
   b. Draw a circle. Shade about 33% of it.
   c. Draw a square. Shade about 90% of it.

8. Draw a line segment. Label one end 0%, and the other end 100%. Show the markings for 20%, 33%, 50%, and 66%.

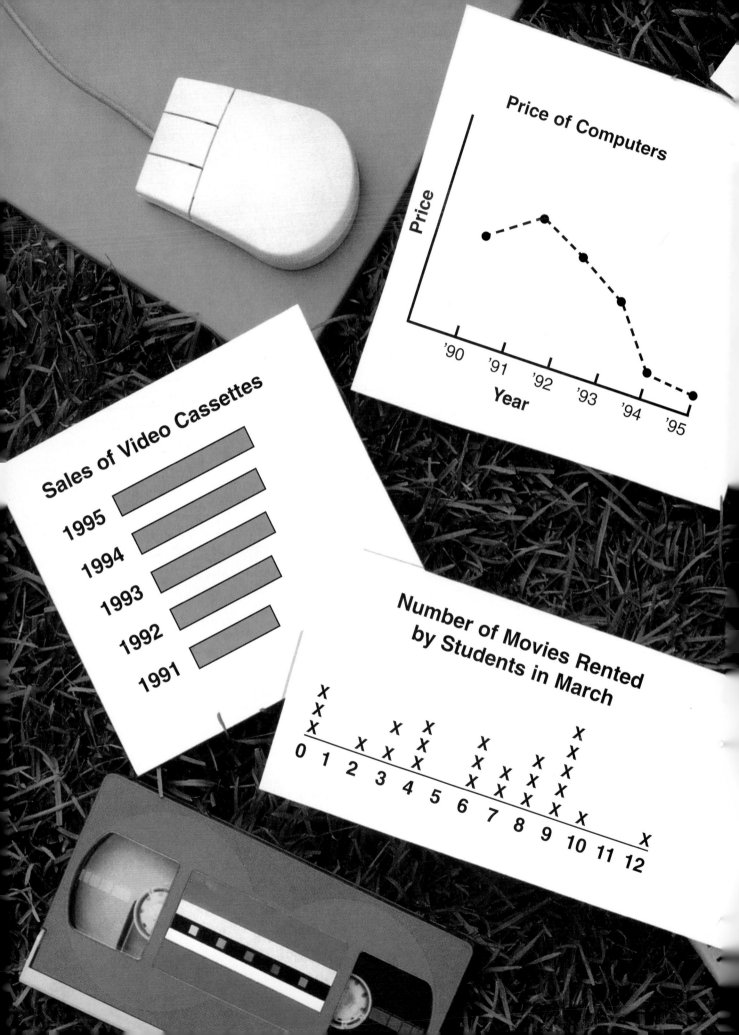

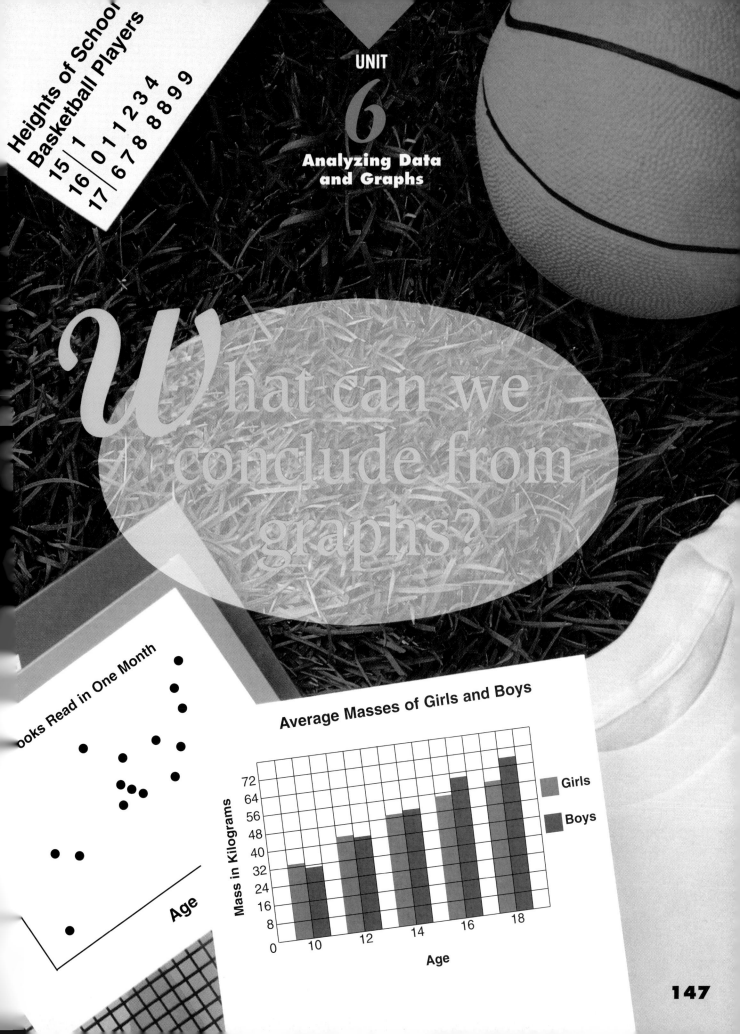

Heights of School Basketball Players

15	1
16	0 1 1 2 3 4
17	6 7 8 8 8 9 9

*W*hat can we conclude from graphs?

Books Read in One Month

Age

Average Masses of Girls and Boys

Mass in Kilograms

72
64
56
48
40
32
24
16
8
0

10   12   14   16   18

Age

Girls

Boys

147

STARTING OUT

1. What equipment might you suggest the rental shop re-stock for next winter?

   a. To answer the question above, what data can you collect about the people in this picture?

   b. Collect data about one group of people in this picture. Present the data clearly in a graph.

   c. What is your answer to the question above? Explain how you made your decision.

   My Journal: When have you had to collect data to make a decision?

ANALYZING DATA AND GRAPHS

S·T·A·R·T·I·N·G·
S OUT

Favourite Winter Activities at Clear Lake Winter Fun Centre

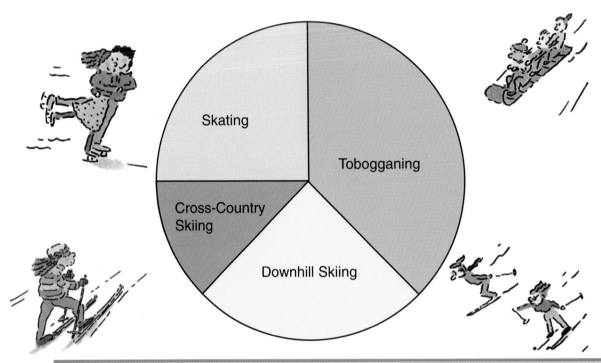

Skating

Tobogganing

Cross-Country Skiing

Downhill Skiing

Number of People Who Rented Equipment at Clear Lake Winter Fun Centre

Skates	Downhill Skis	Toboggans	Cross-Country Skis
	X		
	X		
	X		
	X		X
	X		X
X	X		X
X	X		X
X	X		X
X	X	X	X
X	X	X	X

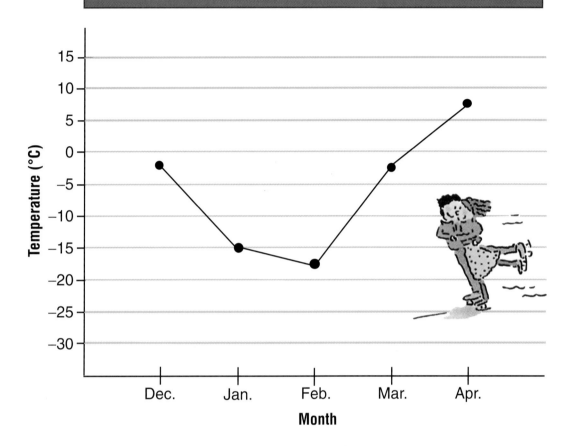

Average Winter Temperatures at Clear Lake Winter Fun Centre

Temperature (°C) vs. Month

2 a. What different types of information are shown in these graphs?

b. What kinds of decisions can be made from the information shown?

c. Choose one graph. Tell everything you can learn from it. 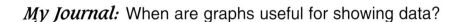 Show the information in another way. Which do you think is clearer? Why?

My Journal: When are graphs useful for showing data?

Understanding Sampling

▶ Each statement on this newspaper page uses data from a sample. Read each statement. Think about who might have been the sample. Also think about whether the sample is representative of the population.

The majority of doctors who use hand lotion prefer **Oceans of lotion**

Most cookie eaters agree, **CRUNCHIES** taste best!

Four fifths of all cocoa drinkers surveyed prefer **LOCO-COCOA** to Choco-Coca

"Three out of four dentists recommend **TASTY TOOTH** Paste."

It's Canada's most popular bicycle for kids between the ages of 10 and 12

We surveyed people between the ages of 18 and 25 to find out the Canada's favourite pizza is **CHECKERS PIZZA**

ON YOUR OWN

▶ Try the hand clasp experiment with people at home or with friends. Copy this table. Tally the results in the table.

Hand Clasping	
Left thumb on top	
Right thumb on top	

1. How many people are in your sample?

2. Describe the results of your sample.

3. For which population are your results a sampling?

4. How do the results of your home sample compare with the results for the class?

5. *My Journal:* Do you think statements made from a sample are always accurate for a population? Explain.

Practise Your Skills

```
  u        n      u       u  u      n       u
 n  u   n     n  u     n            u  n        n
 n        u   u  u  n      u  u  n      n
  u       n  n  u    n      n       u
  n     u            n    n    u      n
 u   n       u  n  n       n     u
```

1. Use a short string to loop five letters.
2. Tally the results of your sample.
3. Predict the results for the total population of 40.
4. Tally the results for the entire population.
5. Compare the results. Was your prediction accurate?

Investigating Sampling

▶ Would these be good ways to select a representative sample from your class? Why or why not?

- your four best friends
- four girls
- four boys
- the first four names in an alphabetical class list
- four people sitting near you

ON YOUR OWN

1. How good are you at predicting?
   a. Choose one of these questions.
      - Do you prefer bicycling or roller blading?
      - Do you prefer to do your homework by yourself or with friends?
      - Do you prefer to take part in sports events or watch?
   b. Decide on a way to select a random sample from your class.
   c. Ask each person in the sample the question. Record the results.
   d. Predict the preference of the whole class.
   e. Survey the class. Compile the results.
   f. Write to explain how accurate your prediction was.

2. *My Journal:* How can you choose a random sample?

Where are you from?

There are people of many different cultures living in Canada today. If you point to any place on the globe, chances are that some people from there are Canadians.

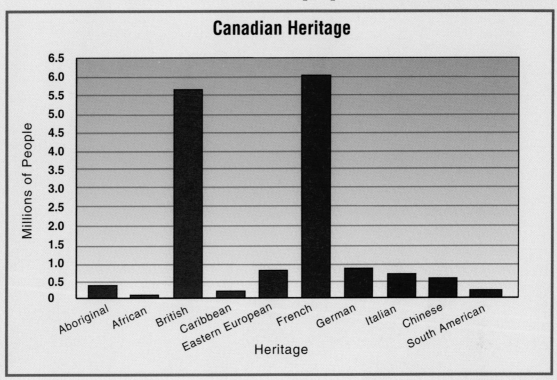

Canadian Heritage

1. What information does the graph present? Why do you think it is presented this way?

2. List two different ways to present the same information.

3. The chart shows the 10 countries from which the greatest number of immigrants came in 1992. How does the information in the graph compare with the information in the chart?

4. Take a class survey to find out everyone's heritage. Graph the results.

Countries of Origin for Immigrants (1992)	
Hong Kong	12.7%
China	10.1%
India	6.5%
Philippines	6.2%
Sri Lanka	5.8%
Poland	5.4%
Vietnam	3.6%
Iran	3.2%
Taiwan	3.1%
Lebanon	3.0%

Analyzing and Investigating Scatterplots

Rashad   Ben   Dave   Lin   Bibi

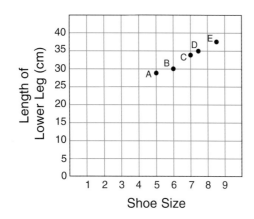

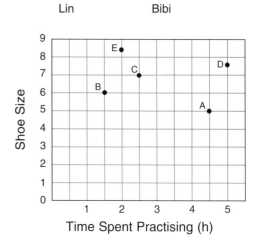

These scatterplots give information about 5 soccer players.

▶ Which player is probably represented by Dot E? Why do you think so? Do you think shoe size is related to length of lower leg? Do you think shoe size is related to practice time? Explain your thinking.

Students kept a record of how much time they spent on the telephone every day for 1 month. They calculated the mean time per day. The results of the survey are shown in the scatterplot.

1. How many students were surveyed? How do you know?

2. How many students say they talk on the phone for more than half an hour a day? How do you know?

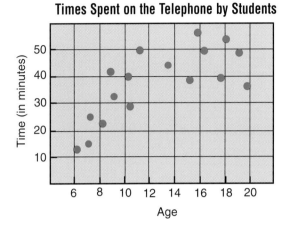

Times Spent on the Telephone by Students

3. How many students under 12 say they talk on the phone for less than 20 minutes a day? How can you tell?

4. Is there a relationship between the age of those surveyed and the amount of time spent talking on the phone? How does the scatterplot show this?

5. *My Journal:* How do scatterplots help you analyze data?

Practise Your Skills

1. Collect data about the heights of objects and the lengths of their shadows. Draw a scatterplot with the data. Is there a relationship between these measurements?

2. Collect data about a grocery store item that comes in 4 or more different-size packages. Record the mass or capacity of each. Record the price of each. Use the data to draw a scatterplot. Is there a relationship between size and price?

Line Plots

A grade 6 class was surveyed. Look at the line plots on this and the next page. Each line plot shows the results for one of the five questions students were asked.

▶ Match each line plot to a question. Explain your reasoning. Then answer the questions on page 159.

1. About how many times do you hiccup before stopping?

2. What is your shoe size?

3. What is the length in seconds of your favourite jingle?

4. What is the mean number of phone calls you make or get in a day?

5. About how many seconds will it take you to count to 100?

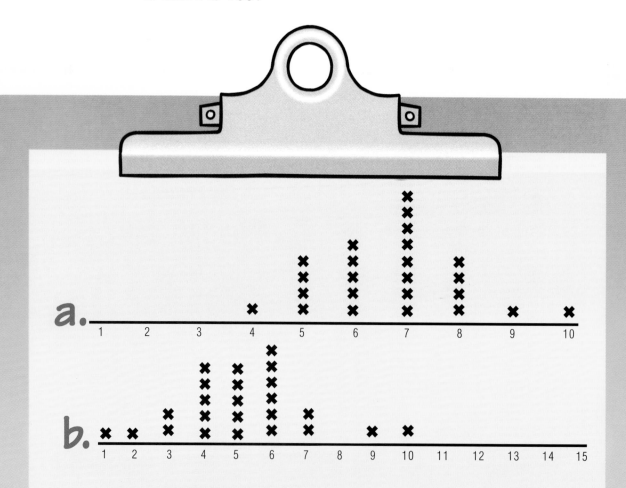

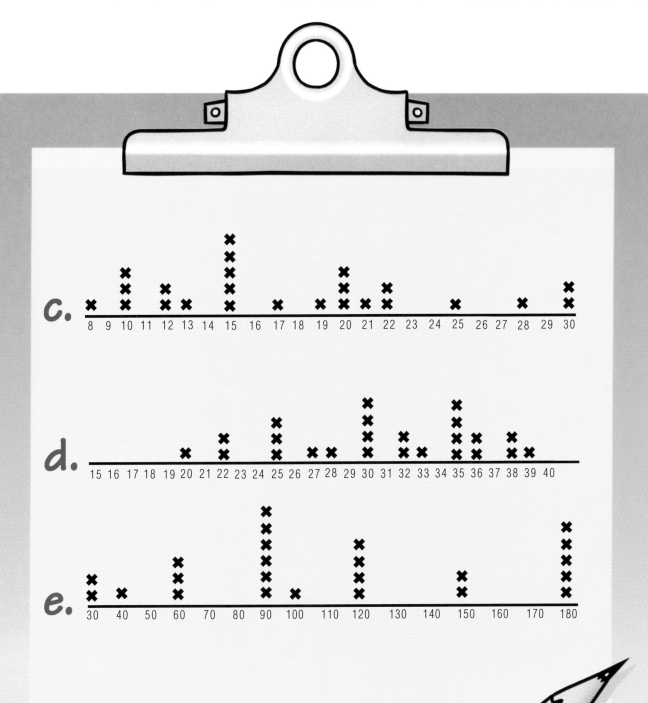

c.

| 8 | 9 | 10 | 11 | 12 | 13 | 14 | 15 | 16 | 17 | 18 | 19 | 20 | 21 | 22 | 23 | 24 | 25 | 26 | 27 | 28 | 29 | 30 |

d.

| 15 | 16 | 17 | 18 | 19 | 20 | 21 | 22 | 23 | 24 | 25 | 26 | 27 | 28 | 29 | 30 | 31 | 32 | 33 | 34 | 35 | 36 | 37 | 38 | 39 | 40 |

e.

| 30 | 40 | 50 | 60 | 70 | 80 | 90 | 100 | 110 | 120 | 130 | 140 | 150 | 160 | 170 | 180 |

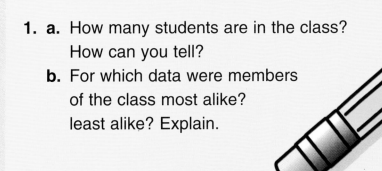

1. a. How many students are in the class?
How can you tell?

b. For which data were members
of the class most alike?
least alike? Explain.

ON YOUR OWN

1. Choose two situations below. For each, collect the data. Make a line plot to represent the data. Write to explain how you collected your data. Write to explain what each line plot shows.

   a. the length of time, in seconds, each classmate spends brushing her or his teeth daily

   b. the number of books each classmate thinks he or she will read in a school year

   c. the number of chocolate chip cookies each classmate says he or she could eat in a sitting

   d. the number of different television programs each classmate says he or she watches on an average day

2. *My Journal:* What do you find most useful about line plots? Why?

Practise Your Skills

Movies Rented in a Month

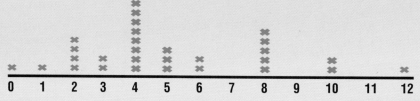

```
                    x
                    x
                    x
                    x
          x         x
          x         x         x
          x    x    x    x    x         x
 x    x   x    x    x    x    x    x         x         x
 0    1   2    3    4    5    6    7    8    9    10   11   12
```

1. What is the range of the data?
2. How many movies were rented?
3. Where do the data cluster?
4. What is the mode for the data?

Double-Bar Graphs

Two groups of students were asked about their favourite leisure activity. The double-bar graph below displays the results of the survey.

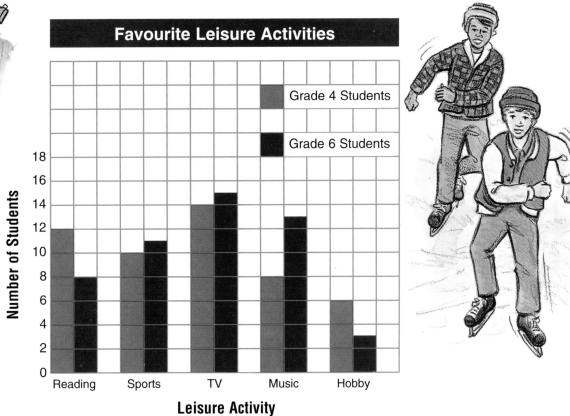

Favourite Leisure Activities

Grade 4 Students

Grade 6 Students

Number of Students

18 16 14 12 10 8 6 4 2 0

Reading Sports TV Music Hobby

Leisure Activity

1. How many students were surveyed?
2. What information does the graph provide?
3. What conclusions can you draw from the graph?
4. Why is it called a double-bar graph?

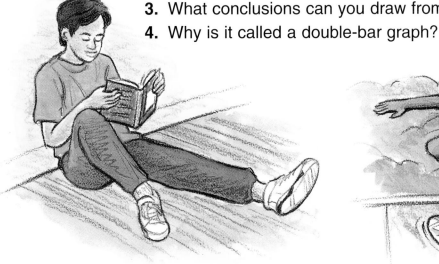

ON YOUR OWN

1. Here are the education levels of Canadians 15 years and older for 1971 and 1991.

EDUCATION LEVELS OF CANADIANS		
	1971	**1991**
Less than Grade 9	32%	14%
Grades 9-12	46%	43%
Some Post-Secondary	17%	32%
University Degree	5%	11%

a. Make a double-bar graph. Display the 2 sets of data.

b. Write all the comparison statements about the graph that you can. Explain any differences you see.

2. Sometimes data can be grouped in intervals. In this case, you can make a *histogram*.

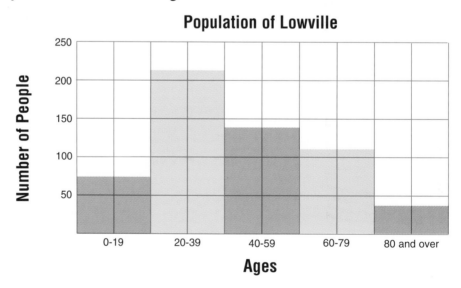

Population of Lowville

a. In the histogram above, how many people are between 0 and 19 years of age?

b. How many people are 40 or older?

c. What else can you learn from this histogram?

3. This table shows the math test scores of a class of grade 6 students.

   a. Draw a histogram to display these data.
   b. How many students scored above 80?
   c. In which interval is the median?

MATH TEST SCORES		
Interval	Number of Students	Frequency
0 – 40		
41 – 50	I	1
51 – 60	II	2
61 – 70	HHT I	6
71 – 80	HHT HHT II	12
81 – 90	HHT III	8
91 – 100	III	3

4. *My Journal:* List some examples of types of data you could display in a double-bar graph. List some examples of types of data you could display in a histogram.

Practise Your Skills

1. A class of grade 6 students wrote an English test. Here are their marks out of 100.

   a. Copy and complete the chart.
   b. Draw a histogram.
   c. The pass mark is 60. How many students passed?
   d. How many students wrote the test?

ENGLISH TEST SCORES		
Interval	Tally	Frequency
20 – 29	II	
30 – 39	II	
40 – 49	IIII	
50 – 59	HHT HHT I	
60 – 69	HHT II	
70 – 79	HHT	
80 – 89	II	
90 – 99	I	

Stem-and-Leaf Plots

José measured the circumferences of 25 maple trees. He made the measurements 1 m above the ground. The results are shown here.

80.6 cm, 80.4 cm, 79.5 cm, 75.9 cm, 80.3 cm, 79.7 cm, 79.0 cm,
75.6 cm, 77.5 cm, 79.2 cm, 80.8 cm, 79.9 cm, 79.5 cm, 81.4 cm,
77.8 cm, 79.0 cm, 77.5 cm, 79.9 cm, 79.8 cm, 77.2 cm, 83.4 cm,
76.8 cm, 78.2 cm, 82.5 cm, 80.5 cm

These data can be arranged on a stem-and-leaf plot.

Stem	Leaves
75.	6 9
76.	8
77.	2 5 5 8
78.	2
79.	0 0 2 5 5 7 8 9 9
80.	3 4 5 6 8
81.	4
82.	5
83.	4

1. What part of each piece of data forms the stem of the plot?
2. What part forms the leaf?
3. Look at the stem-and-leaf plot. What conclusions can you make?
4. What is the median circumference?
5. What is the mode?

Using Graphs to Analyze Data

The table shows years of life expected at birth for people born in the years shown.

Year Born	Life Expectancy	Year Born	Life Expectancy
1920	54.1	1960	69.7
1930	59.7	1970	70.8
1940	62.9	1980	73.7
1950	68.2	1990	75.4

The broken-line graph represents the same data.

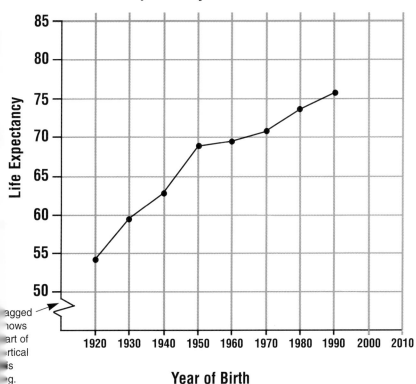

Life Expectancy Based on Year of Birth

The ragged line shows a part of the vertical axis is missing.

1. Predict the life expectancy for someone born in 2000.

2. Suppose a person is born in 2005. About how long is that person expected to live?

3. What information about life expectancy does the graph make easy to see?

4. The increase in life expectancy differs in different 10-year periods. Why do you think this happens?

165

1 What questions does each set of data raise? What kind of graph do you think is most useful for representing the information visually?

2 Choose one set of data. Construct a graph to display the data. Answer the questions it raises.

A.

Education and Mean Monthly Income (1993)

Level of Education	Women	Men
Doctorate	$3162	$4915
Master's Degree	2614	3748
University Graduate	1698	3235
Some University	1115	2002
High School Graduate	943	1853
Some High School	579	1116

B.

Population Density of Canadian Provinces (per km²)

Province	1961	1971	1981	1991
Newfoundland	1.2	1.4	1.5	1.5
Prince Edward Island	18.5	19.7	21.6	22.9
Nova Scotia	14.0	14.9	16.0	17.0
New Brunswick	8.3	8.8	9.7	10.1
Quebec	3.9	4.4	4.7	5.1
Ontario	7.0	8.6	9.4	11.0
Manitoba	1.7	1.8	1.9	2.0
Saskatchewan	1.6	1.6	1.7	1.7
Alberta	2.1	2.5	3.5	4.0
British Columbia	1.8	2.4	3.1	3.7

C.

World Cup Soccer Medal Winners

Year	Winner	Year	Winner
1930	Uruguay	1966	England
1934	Italy	1970	Brazil
1938	Italy	1974	W. Germany
1950	Uruguay	1978	Argentina
1954	W. Germany	1982	Italy
1958	Brazil	1986	Argentina
1962	Brazil	1990	W. Germany
		1994	Brazil

1. This table shows the world population up to the year 2000.

World Population	
Year	Population
1650	550 000 000
1700	610 000 000
1750	760 000 000
1800	950 000 000
1850	1 210 000 000
1900	1 630 000 000
1950	2 520 000 000
2000	6 200 000 000 (predicted)

   a. Decide what kind of graph you can draw to show these data. Draw the graph.
   b. What does your graph tell you about the changing world population? How does it do this?
   c. What do you predict the population will be in the year 2050? Why?

2. Find information about the population of your province or territory since 1900. Graph your data. Use your graph to predict the populations for the years 2000 and 2050.

Brothers and Sisters	
Number of Siblings	Number of Students
0	8
1	5
2	12
3	8
4	3
5	2
6	0

3. Draw a graph or plot for the sibling information shown at the left. What does your graph tell you about the number of siblings each student has? How does it do this?

4. *My Journal:* What type of graph or plot is easiest for you to analyze? What type is easiest for you to construct? Explain.

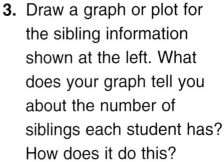

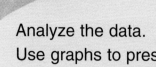

Analyze the data.
Use graphs to present your findings.
Consider scatterplots, broken-line graphs, or line plots. You can use other graphs, such as stem-and-leaf plots, bar graphs, or double-bar graphs.
Write to explain your graphs and why you chose them.

OLYMPIC SUMMER GAMES
100-m Dash
Winning Time (in seconds)

Year	Men	Women
1928	10.8	12.2
1932	10.3	11.9
1936	10.3	11.5
1948	10.3	11.9
1952	10.4	11.5
1956	10.5	11.5
1960	10.2	11.0
1964	10.0	11.4
1968	9.95	11.0
1972	10.14	11.07
1976	10.06	11.08
1980	10.25	11.6
1984	9.99	10.97
1988	9.92	10.54
1992	9.96	10.82

Consider these questions:
1. How can you compare the differences in time for the 100-m dash for men and women?
2. How can you show the changes in times for women to run the 100-m dash from 1928 to 1992?
3. How can you compare the differences in length for the long jump for men and women? the changes in distances jumped by men from 1948 to 1992?
4. Is there a relationship between the numbers of gold and bronze Olympic medals won by a country in the top 20?
5. How can you show what part of the 18 medals that Canada won were gold, silver, and bronze?

LONG JUMP

Distance Year	Men	Women
1948	7.83 m	5.70 m
1952	7.57 m	6.15 m
1956	7.84 m	6.26 m
1960	8.37 m	6.28 m
1964	7.99 m	6.77 m
1968	8.91 m	6.82 m
1972	8.25 m	6.79 m
1976	8.35 m	6.73 m
1980	8.55 m	7.07 m
1984	8.55 m	6.96 m
1988	8.72 m	7.41 m
1992	8.86 m	7.15 m

Olympic Medals Top 20 Countries — 1992

	Gold	Silver	Bronze	Total
Unified Team*	45	38	29	112
United States	37	34	37	108
Germany	33	21	28	82
China	16	22	16	54
Cuba	14	6	11	31
Hungary	11	12	7	30
South Korea	12	5	12	29
France	8	5	16	29
Australia	7	9	11	27
Spain	13	7	2	22
Japan	3	8	11	22
Great Britain	5	3	12	20
Italy	6	5	8	19
Poland	3	6	10	19
Canada	6	5	7	18
Romania	4	6	8	18
Bulgaria	3	7	6	16
Netherlands	2	6	7	15
Sweden	1	7	4	12
New Zealand	1	4	5	10

*Refers to former Soviet Union

CheckYOURSELF

Great Job! You analyzed data and chose appropriate graphs to show your findings. Your graphs were constructed and labelled correctly. You wrote to explain your choice of graphs. Your report was clear and easy to follow.

PROBLEM BANK

1. A random sample is one in which everyone has an equal chance of being chosen. List some ways a random sample can be taken from your school. Explain your thinking.

2. Here is a headline from a local newspaper.

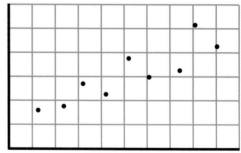

   a. What questions do you think students were asked?
   b. Who do you think the reporters asked?
   c. Do you think statements like this headline are true? Explain your thinking.

3. a. 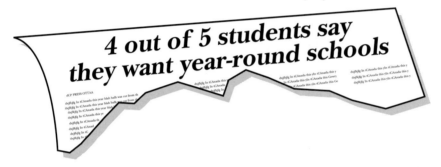 b.

Which scatterplot do you think shows the heights of children of different ages? Explain your reasoning. Suggest suitable numbers and labels you could include on the scatterplot.

4. Students were surveyed about the mean time they spend playing sports every day. The results are shown in this scatterplot.

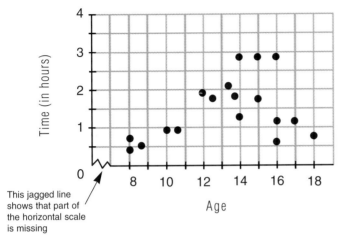

Time (in hours)

Age

This jagged line shows that part of the horizontal scale is missing

   a. How many students were surveyed? How do you know?
   b. How many students said they played sports for more than two hours a day? How do you know?
   c. Is there a relationship between the age of those surveyed and the amount of time spent on sports? How does the scatterplot show this?

5. a. Estimate how long it would take each of 10 students to count to 50. Draw a line plot to show your estimates.
   b. Now ask each of 10 students to count to 50. Use a stopwatch. Draw a second line plot with the results.
   c. In what ways are the plots similar?
   d. In what ways are the plots different?

6. A grade 6 class was surveyed. The survey showed that all 26 students liked potato chips. Seven students liked salt and vinegar flavour. Twice as many liked ketchup flavour. One student liked regular. The remainder were equally split between dill pickle, and sour cream and onion. Draw a line plot to show this information.

7.

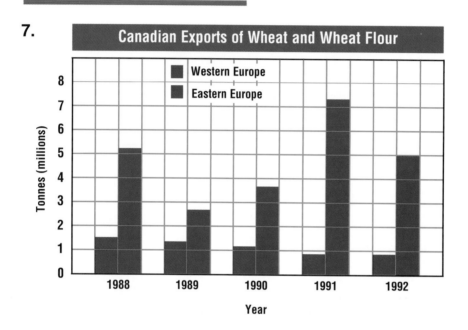

Canadian Exports of Wheat and Wheat Flour

- Western Europe
- Eastern Europe

Tonnes (millions)

1988 1989 1990 1991 1992

Year

a. Describe the change in wheat exports to Western Europe from 1988 to 1992.

b. Describe the change in wheat exports to Eastern Europe from 1988 to 1992. How do you think this affected wheat farmers in Canada?

8. Students in a grade 6 class received these marks on a math test.

62	78	83	90	86	75	93	78	58
76	82	80	85	74	87	83	65	97
77	81	74	82	66	80	78	83	76

a. Make a stem-and-leaf plot to show the marks.

b. What does the stem-and-leaf plot show about the achievement of the students?

c. What is the median mark?

9. a. Suppose you want to display the information in the table. What types of graphs could you use?

b. Draw three different graphs to show this information.

c. Is one type of graph easier to draw? Explain.

d. Is one type of graph easier to understand? Explain.

e. Use your graph. What predictions could you make about TV viewing in the future?

Television Viewing per Person	
Year	Average Number of Hours per Week
1965	7.5
1970	12.4
1975	18.6
1980	23.1
1985	24.1
1990	23.3

10.

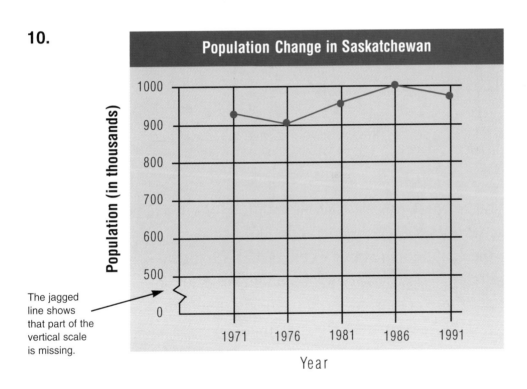

The jagged line shows that part of the vertical scale is missing.

a. What information is shown here?

b. What information is missing that you might find useful? Why would it be useful?

S K I L L BANK

FROM THIS UNIT

1. Here is a scatterplot of André's scores on weekly spelling quizzes. How would you describe his results?

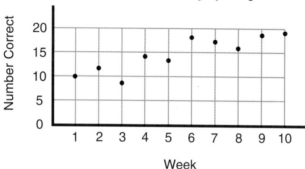

André's Scores on Weekly Spelling Quizzes

Number Correct

Week

2. Suppose you spend some time each day on a sport or doing something active. Draw a broken-line graph for one week to show how many hours a day you spend on that activity.
   a. Are there patterns to your week? What are they?
   b. What predictions can you make about your days?
   c. Suppose you continued the broken-line graph for one month. What kind of information would you get?

3. A cereal company checked the masses of the contents of some 400-g boxes of one of its products. The results, in grams, were:

   398 401   400   405   402   397   405   401
   400 399   400   401   403   395   402   406
   406 407   401   392   399   411   409   401

   a. Make a stem-and-leaf plot of the data.
   b. Where do the data cluster? Are there any outliers?
   c. What is the mode? the median?

1. What is each ratio of circles to triangles?

a.  **b.**  **c.**

2. What percent of each grid is shaded?

a. 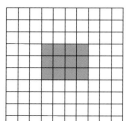 **b.** 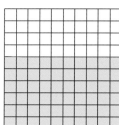 **c.**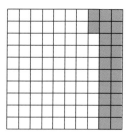

3. Copy and complete. Then write each fraction as a percent.

  a. $\frac{1}{4} = \frac{\blacksquare}{100}$ **b.** $\frac{1}{5} = \frac{\blacksquare}{100}$ **c.** $\frac{4}{5} = \frac{\blacksquare}{100}$ **d.** $\frac{3}{4} = \frac{\blacksquare}{100}$

4. a. About how many hundredths is $\frac{1}{3}$? What percent is that?

  b. About how many hundredths is $\frac{2}{3}$? What percent is that?

5. Draw a circle. Shade part of it. Write a fraction, a decimal, and a percent to label the shaded part.

6. Write each fraction and decimal as a percent.

  a. $\frac{3}{10}$ **b.** $\frac{21}{100}$ **c.** $\frac{1}{4}$ **d.** $\frac{5}{100}$

  e. 0.24 **f.** 0.5 **g.** 0.10 **h.** 0.93

7. Name a fraction, a decimal, and a percent that lie between each pair of numbers.

  a. 0.4 and 50% **b.** $\frac{2}{3}$ and 75% **c.** 0.36 and $\frac{1}{3}$

8. Which is the higher temperature in each pair? Explain.

  a. 0°C or −5°C **b.** −6°C or +3°C **c.** −4°C or −2°C

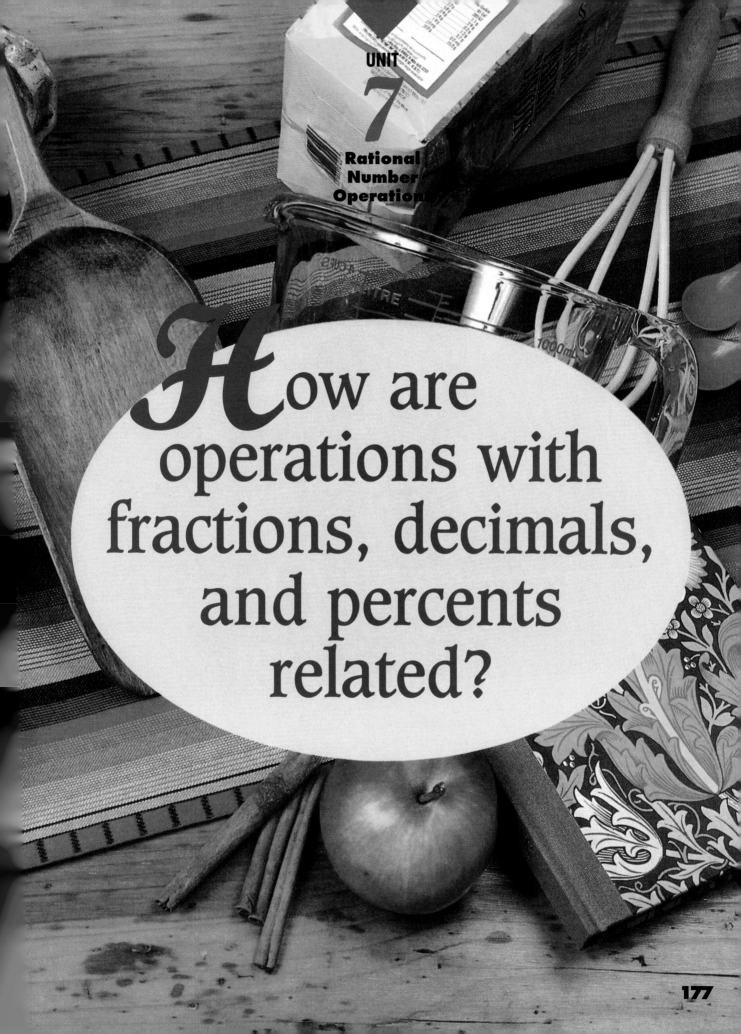

*H*ow are
operations with
fractions, decimals,
and percents
related?

RATIONAL NUMBER
OPERATIONS

S·T·A·R·T·I·N·G·
OUT

Canada has 36 national parks. There is at least one in each province
and territory. The circle graph on page 179 shows the number of parks in
each of the 10 provinces and 2 territories as a fraction of the total
number of parks.

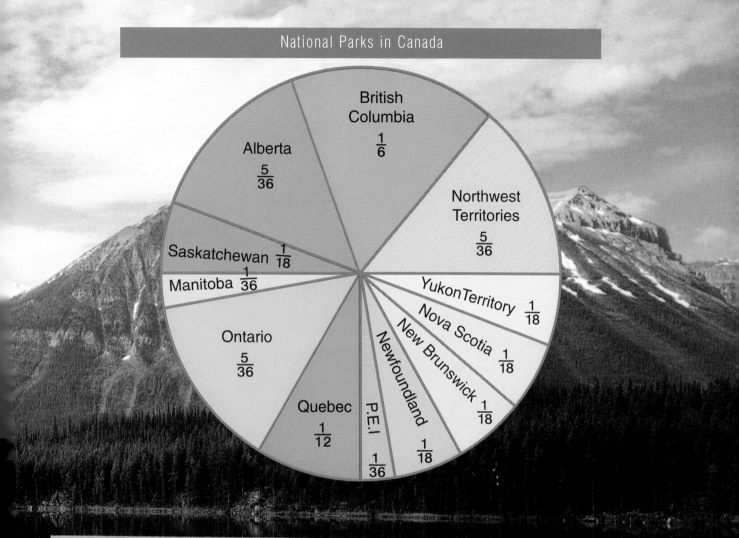

National Parks in Canada

British Columbia $\frac{1}{6}$

Alberta $\frac{5}{36}$

Northwest Territories $\frac{5}{36}$

Saskatchewan $\frac{1}{18}$

Manitoba $\frac{1}{36}$

Yukon Territory $\frac{1}{18}$

Nova Scotia $\frac{1}{18}$

New Brunswick $\frac{1}{18}$

Newfoundland $\frac{1}{18}$

Ontario $\frac{5}{36}$

Quebec $\frac{1}{12}$

P.E.I $\frac{1}{36}$

1 Name a set of provinces or territories that together have about $\frac{1}{4}$ of the national parks.

2 Name two provinces that together have as many parks as Quebec. Name three provinces that together have as many parks as British Columbia.

3 British Columbia has $\frac{1}{6}$ of the 36 national parks. About how many is that? Explain how you know.

My Journal: What do you know about adding and subtracting fractions? What do you still want to know?

RATIONAL NUMBER
OPERATIONS

STARTING
OUT

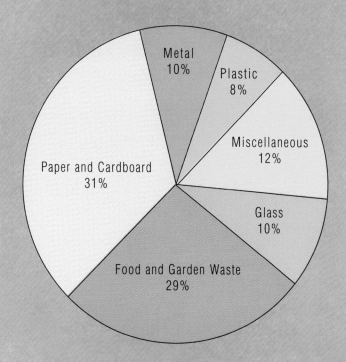

Most families produce between 20 kg and 45 kg of garbage each week.

4 How much garbage would a family produce in one day? in three days?

5 Express each percent on the graph as a fraction, then as a decimal.

6 Which garbage type is produced in about the same percent as paper and cardboard?

7 Which garbage types are about $\frac{1}{3}$ the percent of paper and cardboard?

8 Is 12% closer to $\frac{1}{5}$ or $\frac{1}{10}$? How do you know?

9 What percent would you use to describe a little more than one half? a little less than $\frac{3}{4}$? about $\frac{1}{4}$? almost none? almost all?

My Journal: What do the words *fraction*, *decimal*, and *percent* mean? How are fractions, decimals, and percents related?

Combining Fractions and Mixed Numbers

▶ How many ads can you fit on a page?

Advertising Rates

Space	Cost
$\frac{1}{8}$	$125
$\frac{1}{4}$	$235
$\frac{1}{2}$	$450
$\frac{3}{4}$	$775
Full page	$875

1 page of ads pays for about 6 magazine pages

ON YOUR OWN

1. The magazine editor has asked you to do a layout for a page. The page has a $\frac{1}{2}$ page ad and a $\frac{1}{8}$ page ad. How many different ways can you make a page that has ads these sizes? Draw sketches to show your thinking.

2. Use the data on page 182. Show as many different ways as you can to use a full page of ads. Which costs the least for the advertiser? Which costs the most?

3. The second week the magazine was in business, it sold a total of $5\frac{1}{2}$ pages of ads. This was twice as much as in the first week. How many pages of ads were sold the first week? How many were sold in both weeks combined?

4. *My Journal:* What did you learn about combining fractions and mixed numbers? What would you still like to learn?

Practise Your Skills

1. Find each sum.

   a. $\frac{1}{5} + \frac{2}{5}$ b. $\frac{3}{8} + \frac{2}{8}$

   c. $\frac{1}{6} + \frac{1}{6}$ d. $\frac{3}{10} + \frac{4}{10}$

2. Find each sum. Write the sum as a whole number or a mixed number.

   a. $\frac{1}{2} + \frac{1}{2}$ b. $\frac{3}{4} + \frac{3}{4}$ c. $\frac{7}{8} + \frac{5}{8}$

   d. $\frac{3}{5} + \frac{2}{5}$ e. $3\frac{1}{6} + \frac{4}{6}$ f. $1\frac{1}{2} + 1\frac{1}{2}$

   g. $4\frac{3}{10} + 2\frac{4}{10}$ h. $2\frac{1}{4} + \frac{3}{4}$

What's for DINNER?

Have you ever wondered what kinds of foods people eat in different parts of the world? One important food is rice. Rice is popular in many parts of Asia, Africa, Central America, and the Caribbean. Here are two different rice recipes. One is from Japan. The other is from the Caribbean. Try making them with a friend.

When people cook, they often use imperial measures. The recipes here show both imperial and metric measures.

Rinse the rice in a strainer under cold water, then drain it. Put the 375 mL water in a heavy pot and bring it to a boil. Put in the rice, cover the pot, and cook over very low heat for 15 minutes. Turn off the heat. Stir in the vinegar, sugar, and salt. Let the pot sit covered for another 15 minutes. This makes four servings.

Sushi Rice

375 mL	short-grain rice	$1\frac{1}{2}$ cups
375 mL	water	$1\frac{1}{2}$ cups
125 mL	rice vinegar	$\frac{1}{2}$ cup
45 mL	sugar	3 tablespoons
10 mL	salt	2 teaspoons

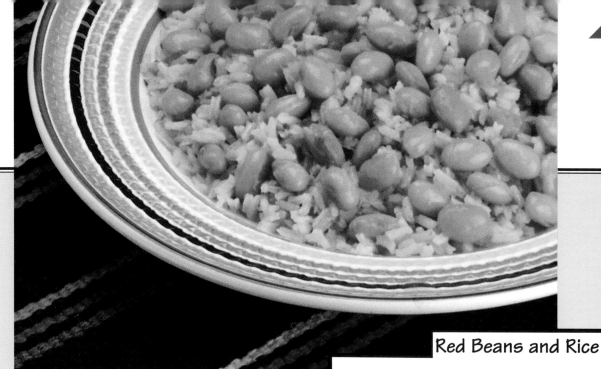

Rinse the rice in a strainer under cold water, then drain it. Put the rice in a heavy pot, add the 500 mL water, and bring it to a boil over high heat. Then turn down the heat to very low, cover the pot, and cook for 12 minutes. Take pot off the heat and let it sit for five minutes.

While the rice is cooking, place the red beans in a strainer. Rinse them with very hot water and then drain them. Stir them into the cooked rice and add the salt and pepper. This makes four servings.

Red Beans and Rice

375 mL	long-grain rice	$1\frac{1}{2}$ cups
500 mL	water	2 cups
500 mL	cooked red beans	2 cups
1 mL	salt	$\frac{1}{4}$ teaspoon
1 mL	pepper	$\frac{1}{4}$ teaspoon

1 Both of these recipes make 4 servings. What would you do if you wanted to make 8 servings of each? What would you do if you wanted to make 2 servings of each?

2 What would you do if you wanted to make enough of each recipe to serve half your class?

3 How do you like your rice cooked? Make a class recipe book with everyone's favourite rice recipes. Try a recipe that is new to you and see how you like it.

Using Fractions and Decimals

1. Find the area of each rectangle.

a.
2 units
3 units

b.
2 units
$3\frac{1}{2}$ units

c.
2 units
3.25 units

2. Compare Don's and Judith's hikes.

a. Judith walked 4 hours on Saturday and Don walked 6 hours. How much longer did Don walk than Judith?

b. Judith completed a certain hiking trail in $4\frac{1}{2}$ hours. It took Don 6 hours to hike the same trail. How much longer did it take Don than Judith to complete the hike?

c. On Wednesday, Judith took 4.5 hours to walk the trail and Don took 6 hours. How much longer did it take Don than Judith?

3. How many recipes of trail mix can you make?

a. One recipe calls for 3 scoops of raisins. You have 6 scoops.

b. One recipe calls for $1\frac{1}{2}$ packages. You have 6 packages.

c. One recipe calls for 1.5 kg. You have 6 kg.

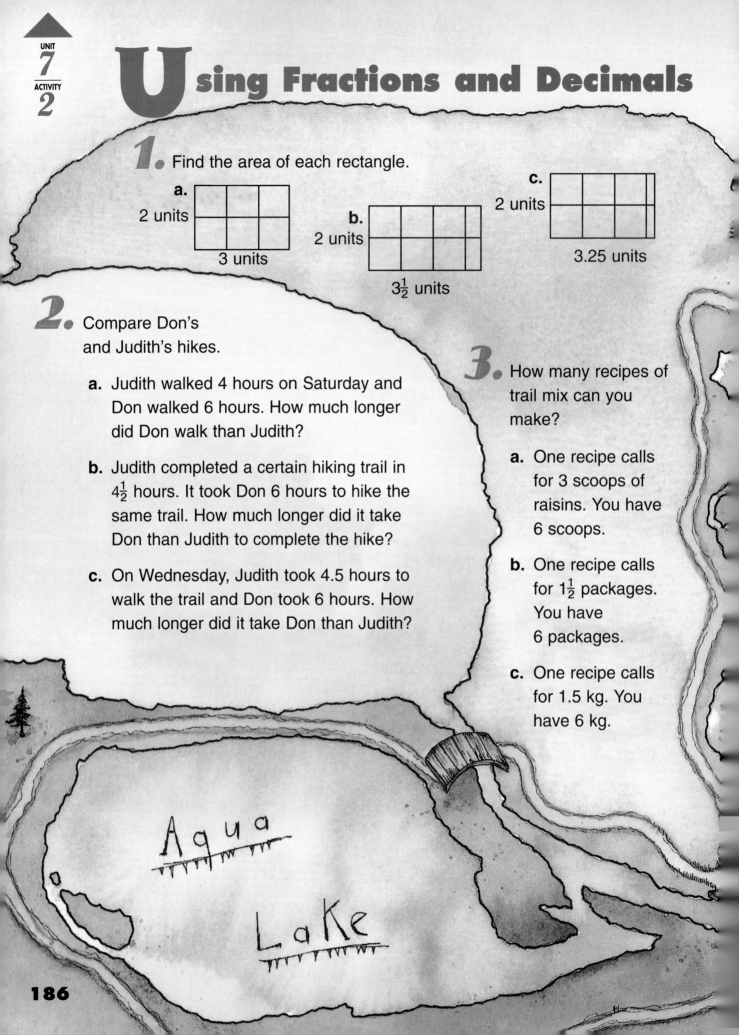

Aqua Lake

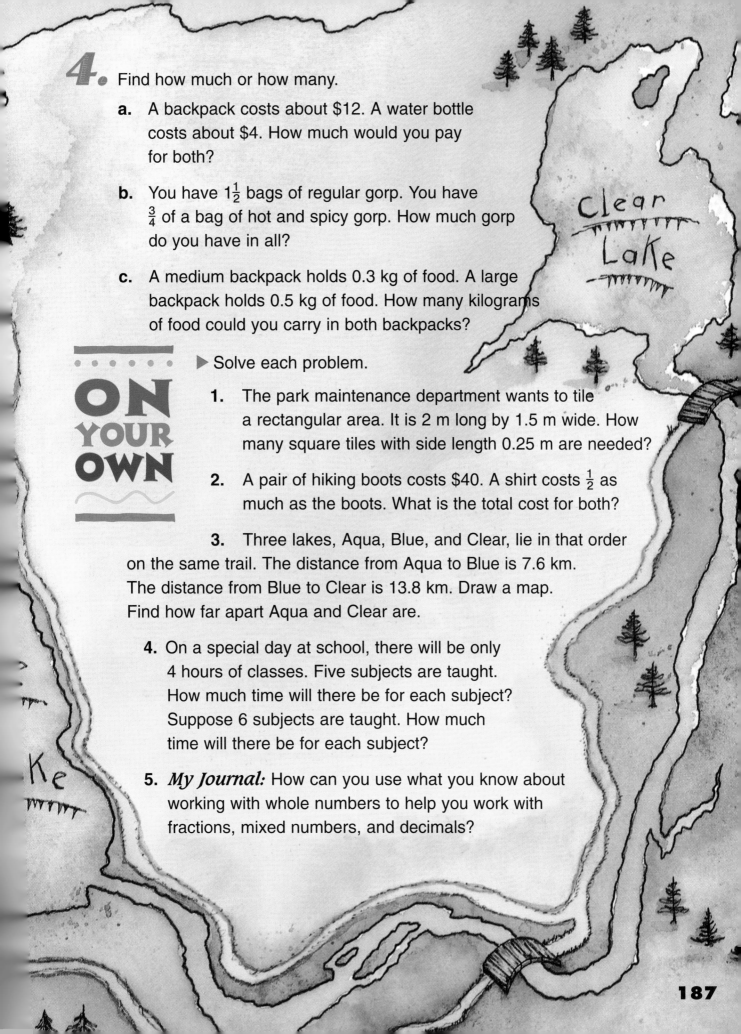

4. Find how much or how many.

a. A backpack costs about $12. A water bottle costs about $4. How much would you pay for both?

b. You have $1\frac{1}{2}$ bags of regular gorp. You have $\frac{3}{4}$ of a bag of hot and spicy gorp. How much gorp do you have in all?

c. A medium backpack holds 0.3 kg of food. A large backpack holds 0.5 kg of food. How many kilograms of food could you carry in both backpacks?

ON YOUR OWN

▶ Solve each problem.

1. The park maintenance department wants to tile a rectangular area. It is 2 m long by 1.5 m wide. How many square tiles with side length 0.25 m are needed?

2. A pair of hiking boots costs $40. A shirt costs $\frac{1}{2}$ as much as the boots. What is the total cost for both?

3. Three lakes, Aqua, Blue, and Clear, lie in that order on the same trail. The distance from Aqua to Blue is 7.6 km. The distance from Blue to Clear is 13.8 km. Draw a map. Find how far apart Aqua and Clear are.

4. On a special day at school, there will be only 4 hours of classes. Five subjects are taught. How much time will there be for each subject? Suppose 6 subjects are taught. How much time will there be for each subject?

5. *My Journal:* How can you use what you know about working with whole numbers to help you work with fractions, mixed numbers, and decimals?

187

Adding and Subtracting Fractions

How did these students add and subtract
fractions and mixed numbers?

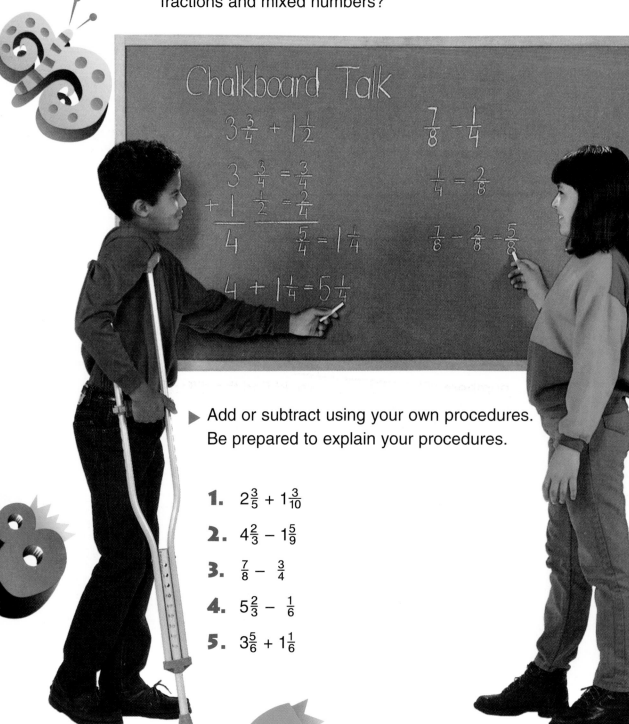

Chalkboard Talk

$3\frac{3}{4} + 1\frac{1}{2}$

$3\ \ \frac{3}{4} = \frac{3}{4}$
$+1\ \ \frac{1}{2} = \frac{2}{4}$
_____
$4\ \ \ \ \ \ \frac{5}{4} = 1\frac{1}{4}$

$4 + 1\frac{1}{4} = 5\frac{1}{4}$

$\frac{7}{8} - \frac{1}{4}$

$\frac{1}{4} = \frac{2}{8}$

$\frac{7}{8} - \frac{2}{8} = \frac{5}{8}$

▶ Add or subtract using your own procedures.
Be prepared to explain your procedures.

1. $2\frac{3}{5} + 1\frac{3}{10}$

2. $4\frac{2}{3} - 1\frac{5}{9}$

3. $\frac{7}{8} - \frac{3}{4}$

4. $5\frac{2}{3} - \frac{1}{6}$

5. $3\frac{5}{6} + 1\frac{1}{6}$

ON YOUR OWN

1. Make up an addition expression with fractions that have different denominators. Show how you would find the sum.

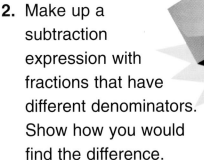

2. Make up a subtraction expression with fractions that have different denominators. Show how you would find the difference.

3. Make up an addition expression with mixed numbers. Show how you would find the sum.

4. Make up a subtraction expression with mixed numbers. Show how you would find the difference.

5. *My Journal:* How do you check your work?

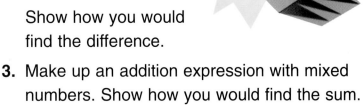

Practise Your Skills

1. Find each sum.

   a. $\frac{1}{8} + \frac{1}{4}$ b. $2\frac{1}{2} + \frac{1}{4}$ c. $4\frac{1}{8} + 2\frac{1}{4}$

   d. $1\frac{3}{4} + 2\frac{1}{2}$ e. $\frac{7}{8} + \frac{2}{4}$ f. $5\frac{2}{3} + 1\frac{1}{6}$

2. Find each difference.

   a. $\frac{5}{8} - \frac{1}{2}$ b. $\frac{3}{4} - \frac{1}{2}$ c. $3\frac{5}{6} - 1\frac{2}{3}$

   d. $4\frac{4}{5} - \frac{2}{5}$ e. $6\frac{1}{2} - 1\frac{1}{3}$ f. $3\frac{5}{8} - 2\frac{1}{4}$

189

Using Decimals

A welder is making a special chain for hanging a lamp. She follows a pattern that alternates two different-sized links. The inside lengths of the links are 4.6 cm and 2.9 cm.

▶ Suppose she wants to make the chain 3.75 m long. How many links of each size would she need?

ON YOUR OWN

▶ Solve these problems.

1. Suppose the welder makes a 2.3-m chain. She uses only the 4.6-cm links. How many links would she need? How can you figure this out?

2. Suppose you ask for a necklace made from the smaller links. You want the necklace to be long enough to slip over your head. Determine a reasonable length for the necklace. Find the number of links needed.

3. Make up a different design for a chain. Use the two kinds of links. Decide on a chain length between 2 m and 3 m. How many of each kind of link will you need?

4. *My Journal:* What did you learn about operations with decimal numbers? What would you still like to learn?

Practise Your Skills

1. Find each sum or difference.
   a. 3.7 + 2.6   **b.** 0.5 + 1.4   **c.** 4.1 + 4.9

   d. 8.6 − 0.5   **e.** 3.7 − 1.2   **f.** 9.1 − 3.3

2. Find each product or quotient.
   a. 4.6 × 8   **b.** 3.1 × 6   **c.** 12.5 × 3

   d. 7.5 ÷ 5   **e.** 8.4 ÷ 4   **f.** 15.9 ÷ 3

Fractions, Decimals, and Percents

▶ Read each advertisement. Estimate how much you would save by buying the item on sale. Estimate the sale price of the item. Then find the amount you would save and the sale price of the item.

1. What is the sale price?

REGULAR PRICE $2.79

ALL ITEMS 50% OFF

2. How much do the socks cost?

ORIGINAL PRICE $4.95

NOW 50% OFF

3. Buy one ticket. Get another ticket at $\frac{2}{3}$ off. What is the price of the second ticket?

2ND ticket $\frac{2}{3}$ OFF

All rides $6.75

All Day!

4. What's the price of the burger?

REGULAR PRICE $3.99

BURGER SURPRISE $\frac{3}{4}$ OFF

5. Is the jewellery free?

REGULARLY $40.00

ALREADY REDUCED 50%

TODAY 50% MORE OFF

6. The original price is $79.50. What is the sale price?

25% OFF

$79.50

HOOKED ON CULUS

1. Look at the calculators on the right. Which calculator costs the least? Explain why.

2. Which is greater: 10% of $1000 or 100% of $100? Explain.

3. This week, a discount store advertises that its merchandise is on sale at 50% off. Every week after this, the merchandise will be reduced by an additional 10%. What is the price of a $100 portable radio this week? What will the price be next week? Will the price ever be $0? Explain.

4. A microwave oven originally cost $200. Last week it was on sale at 50% off. What was its sale price? This week, the price of the microwave was reduced by a further 50%. What is the sale price now? Explain.

5. *My Journal:* Suppose the amount of savings is given as a fraction or percent. Explain how to find the price you must pay for an item.

Practise Your Skills

Solve.

1. 100% of $10	**2.** 50% of $10	**3.** 10% of $10
4. 20% of $100	**5.** 20% of $50	**6.** 20% of $200
7. 60% of $200	**8.** 50% of $125	**9.** 40% of $68
10. 30% of $72	**11.** 25% of $12	**12.** 75% of $75

Using Percents to Compare Data

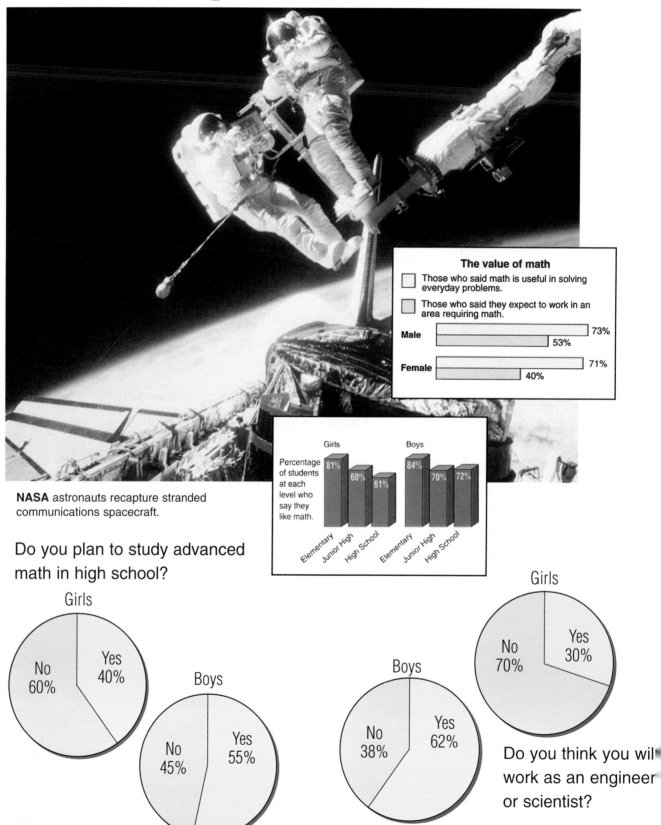

NASA astronauts recapture stranded communications spacecraft.

The value of math

☐ Those who said math is useful in solving everyday problems.

▨ Those who said they expect to work in an area requiring math.

Male 73%
53%

Female 71%
40%

Percentage of students at each level who say they like math.

Girls
81% 68% 61%

Boys
84% 70% 72%

Elementary Junior High High School Elementary Junior High High School

Do you plan to study advanced math in high school?

Girls
No 60% Yes 40%

Boys
No 45% Yes 55%

Boys
No 38% Yes 62%

Girls
No 70% Yes 30%

Do you think you will work as an engineer or scientist?

ON YOUR OWN

1. In a survey, 50 people were asked whether they use math in their work. Forty of them said yes. What fraction is that? How can you write the fraction as a percent?

2. Of the 400 students enrolled in the first year at a medical school, 280 are female. What fraction is that? What percent is that?

3. In a survey, 1000 people were asked if they thought it was very important to know mathematics. The results are shown on the right. How many people thought it was very important?

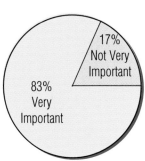

Importance of Mathematics

4. A sample of 2204 high school students was taken. The students were asked if they were interested in a career in business. Look at the circle graph below. About how many students said they were interested in a career in business?

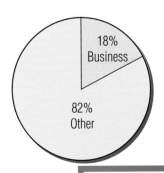

Business Career

5. *My Journal:* How do you decide whether a solution to a problem involving percent is reasonable?

Practise Your Skills

Give each answer first as a fraction, then as a percent.

1. 100 in all: what part is 35?

2. 80 in all: what part is 60?

3. 48 in all: what part is 24?

4. 500 in all: what part is 100?

5. 250 in all: what part is 200?

6. 400 in all: what part is 150?

PIONEER PICNIC

- For each recipe, poll your classmates to find out what percent would want to have it for a picnic.

- If a recipe is chosen by at least 75% of the class, decide how to adjust the recipe to serve the whole class.

- Compute the costs at today's prices (shown beside each ingredient).

CABBAGE SALAD
Makes 10 servings

$\frac{1}{2}$ of a head of cabbage	$0.50
1 onion	$0.13
2 dessert spoons of sugar	$0.02
1$\frac{1}{2}$ dessert spoons of vinegar	$0.06
$\frac{3}{4}$ of a gill of sour cream	$0.28

*1 gill = 120mL

DANDELION AND LETTUCE SALAD
Makes 8 servings

a head of lettuce	$1.29	1$\frac{1}{2}$ dessert spoons of flour	$0.03
4 good handsful of dandelion greens	$1.29	a good sprinkle of salt and pepper	$0.02
2 small onions	$0.26	2 dessert spoons of vinegar	$0.08
2 eggs boiled hard	$0.22	2$\frac{1}{2}$ dessert spoons of sugar	$0.03
$\frac{1}{2}$ of a green pepper	$0.50	1$\frac{1}{2}$ gills of fresh cream	$1.00
5 slices of bacon	$1.00	2 medium tomatoes	$1.25

BUBBLE AND SQUEAK
Makes 8 servings

cold boiled pork butt	$7.00
$\frac{1}{2}$ of a cabbage	$0.50
6 carrots	$0.45
a lump of butter the size of a butternut	$0.10

SALEMA'S GOOD POTATO SALAD
Makes 6 servings

6 medium potatoes	$1.00	a lump of brown sugar the size of a walnut
1$\frac{1}{2}$ onions	$0.35	$\frac{1}{2}$ of a gill of vinegar
2 stalks of celery	$0.22	$\frac{1}{3}$ of a gill of good fresh cream
1 clove garlic	$0.20	
1 egg beaten well	$0.11	

APPLE BETTY
Makes 6 servings

6 apples $1.85
1/2 of a teacup of butter $0.70
a good sprinkle of cinnamon $0.03
2/3 of a cup of brown sugar $0.35
3/4 of a cup of flour $0.12

HONEY CHICKEN
Makes 6 servings

1 medium chicken
a lump of butter
the size of an egg $5.0
1 1/2 gills of honey $0.55
2 scallions $1.15
the juice of 1/2 lemon $0.15
$0.17

EVE'S BREAD PUDDING
Makes 4 or 5 servings

$1.85
$0.45
$0.66
6 apples $0.30
5 thick slices of bread $0.11
6 eggs $0.04
3/4 of a teacup of sugar $0.50
2 good handful of raisins
1/2 of a dessert spoon of nutmeg
2 1/2 gills of milk

Check YOURSELF

Great Job! You found which pioneer recipes were chosen by at least 75% of your classmates. Then you chose a menu for the picnic. You adjusted the recipes so they would serve your class. You computed the cost of ingredients, at today's prices. You wrote to explain why you chose the menu you did and how you found the amounts needed for your class.

RATIONAL NUMBER OPERATIONS

PROBLEM BANK

1. Mark is knitting a sweater. He needs 8 balls of blue yarn, 5 balls of white, $1\frac{1}{2}$ balls of yellow, and $1\frac{1}{4}$ balls of pink.

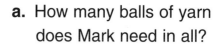

    a. How many balls of yarn does Mark need in all?

    b. Mark has $\frac{1}{2}$ ball of pink from another project. How much more pink does he need?

2. The Jordans went to a pick-your-own apple orchard.

    a. Terry picked $2\frac{1}{2}$ tubs of Northern Spy apples; Lisa and Josh each picked $1\frac{1}{2}$ tubs. How many tubs of apples did they pick in all?

    b. Pierre picked $1\frac{1}{2}$ tubs of Macintosh apples. He used $\frac{3}{4}$ of a tub for pies. How many tubs were left?

3. a. Randolf baby-sits for a neighbour. Calculate how many hours he baby-sits in all from these time periods:

- from 7:00 p.m. to 11:00 p.m.
- from 6:30 p.m. to 7:00 p.m.
- from 4:15 p.m. to 8:00 p.m.
- from 8:30 p.m. to 12:45 a.m.

b. Randolf is paid $3 an hour. How much money did he earn?

c. Randolf spent $\frac{1}{2}$ of his baby-sitting money on a new compact disc. He spent $\frac{1}{3}$ of his money on a movie. He put the rest in the bank. What fraction of his money did he put in the bank?

4. a. Bernice practised the flute for $1\frac{1}{4}$ hours on Monday, $1\frac{1}{4}$ hours on Wednesday, and $\frac{1}{2}$ an hour on Friday. How many hours did Bernice practise that week?

b. This week, Bernice practised for a total of $5\frac{1}{4}$ hours; $2\frac{3}{4}$ hours of that was on the weekend. How much did she practise on weekdays?

5. Rachpal delivers a newspaper to 75 homes. Of these, $\frac{1}{3}$ are on Baycrest Avenue and $\frac{1}{5}$ are on Chelsey Drive. What fraction of the 75 homes does this represent? What fraction of Rachpal's deliveries are on other streets?

6. Chantel had 18 coins in her pocket. One half of them were dimes. One third were nickels. The rest of them were quarters. How much money did Chantel have?

PROBLEM BANK

Use your own procedures to solve these problems. Explain the procedures to a friend.

7. Yin has a model railway.
   Its passenger cars
   are each 10.8 cm long.
   The baggage car is 10.2 cm long.
   The caboose is 7.6 cm long.
   All measures include the coupling.

   a. What is the length of two passenger cars together? Suppose Yin hooks 6 passenger cars together. What is the length?

   b. One of Yin's trains without the engine is 71.2 cm long. With the engine, the train is 80.7 cm long. What is the length of the engine?

   c. Yin made a train 59.7 cm long. Which cars could make up this train?

8. A sporting goods store is having a giant end-of-season sale. All the prices have been reduced. Look at each price tag. What is the sale price of each item?

9. Jill saved $12 by buying her jacket on sale. The regular price was $40.

a. How much did Jill pay?

b. Was the jacket marked 20% off, 30% off, or 40% off?

10. In a survey of 325 students, 44% of them said they were interested in learning self-defence. About how many students did this represent?

11. The 1991 Census of Agriculture in Canada showed that 26% of farmers were women. There are 391 000 farmers in Canada. About how many female farmers are there?

Canadian Farmers

Female Farmers

Male Farmers

12. Ana surveyed 20 classmates. She found that 5 of them have a cat, 4 have a dog, 1 has a hamster, and 1 has a gerbil.

a. What fraction of Ana's classmates have a cat? What percent is that?

b. What percent of Ana's classmates have a dog?

c. What percent of Ana's classmates have either a hamster or a gerbil?

d. What percent of Ana's classmates do not have any of these pets?

S K I L L BANK
FROM THIS UNIT

1. Find each sum.

a. $\frac{1}{3} + \frac{1}{3}$ **b.** $\frac{5}{8} + \frac{1}{8}$ **c.** $\frac{4}{5} + \frac{3}{5}$ **d.** $\frac{1}{2} + \frac{3}{4}$

e. $2\frac{3}{8} + \frac{7}{8}$ **f.** $1\frac{1}{3} + 1\frac{1}{2}$ **g.** $3\frac{3}{10} + \frac{7}{10}$ **h.** $4\frac{5}{6} + 3\frac{1}{3}$

2. Find each difference.

a. $\frac{7}{10} - \frac{3}{10}$ **b.** $\frac{4}{5} - \frac{1}{10}$ **c.** $\frac{5}{6} - \frac{1}{2}$ **d.** $\frac{5}{8} - \frac{1}{4}$

e. $3\frac{1}{4} - 1\frac{1}{4}$ **f.** $4\frac{1}{2} - 2\frac{1}{4}$ **g.** $7\frac{4}{5} - 2\frac{1}{5}$ **h.** $8\frac{3}{5} - 6\frac{1}{10}$

3. Find each sum or difference.

a. $4.3 + 2.6$ **b.** $5.7 + 3.8$ **c.** $12.5 + 4.7$

d. $5.9 - 1.8$ **e.** $16.2 - 8.5$ **f.** $15.3 - 9.6$

4. Find each product or quotient.

a. 7.2×4 **b.** 8.3×5 **c.** 12.5×6

d. $10.5 \div 5$ **e.** $3.4 \div 2$ **f.** $12.6 \div 3$

5. Solve.

a. 50% of $50 **b.** 10% of $20 **c.** 25% of $44

d. 30% of $150 **e.** 20% of $180 **f.** 50% of $25

6. Give each answer first as a fraction, then as a percent.

a. 200 in all: what part is 50? **b.** 40 in all: what part is 20?

c. 150 in all: what part is 30? **d.** 50 in all: what part is 42?

SKILL BANK
LOOKING BACK

1. Write a fraction, a decimal, and a percent for the shaded part of each grid.

a. 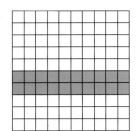   **b.** 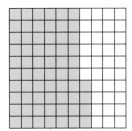   **c.**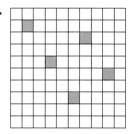

2. Write each fraction or decimal as a percent.

    a. $\frac{1}{5}$ **b.** $\frac{7}{10}$ **c.** $\frac{81}{100}$ **d.** $\frac{3}{100}$

    e. 0.2   **f.** 0.14   **g.** 0.72   **h.** 0.99

3. Which number in each pair is greater? Use the number line to help you.

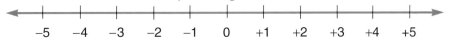

    a. +3 or +5   **b.** +2 or −1   **c.** 0 or −3

    d. +4 or 0   **e.** −5 or +5   **f.** −2 or −4

4. A highway may be built near the edge of Hugo's town. Hugo surveyed the people on his block to find out if they were in favour of it. Was this a random sample? Explain.

5. A music teacher made this line plot. It showed the number of hours her students practised in a week.

    a. What is the range of the data?

    b. Where do the data cluster?

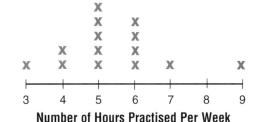

6. Here are the heights (in centimetres) for the standing high jump for a grade 6 class: 73, 84, 68, 91, 80, 82, 76, 75, 85, 95, 89, 81, 77, 75, 80, 81, 79, 81. Make a stem-and-leaf plot of the data. What is the median jump?

OLD TUCSON STUDIOS

PRODUCTION _____

DIRECTOR _____

CAMERA _____   TAKE

DATE   SCENE

SW

MADE IN U.S.A.

METRIC   INCHES 1

How can we analyze, measure, and draw angles?

**MEASURING AND
ANALYZING ANGLES**

STARTING OUT

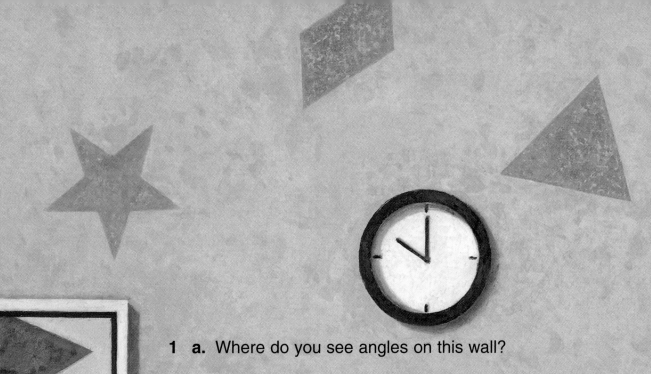

1 a. Where do you see angles on this wall?

b. Which angles do you think are alike?

c. Suppose angles were always like those at the corners of the door. How different would our world look?

My Journal: How are all angles the same?

Words to Know

Angle:
An angle is formed by two rays with the same endpoint.
The endpoint is called the vertex.

ray

ray

vertex

Identifying and Comparing Angles

▶ Look around you to find examples of many types of angles.

▶ Use your angle measurer to find congruent angles in this scene. Write to describe what you found.

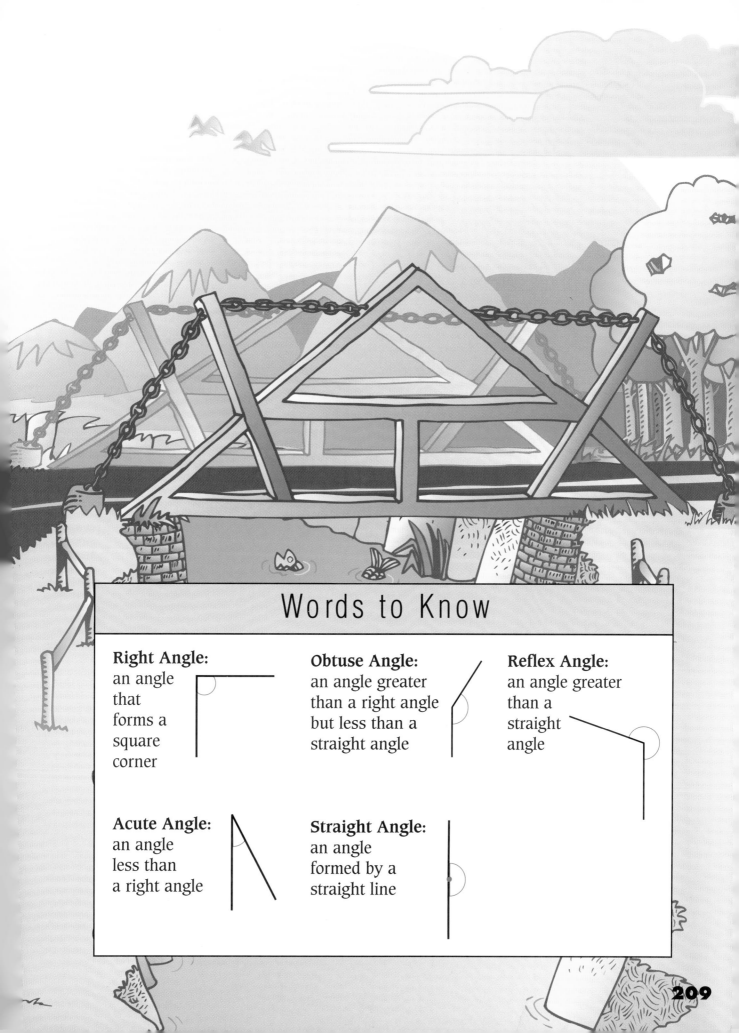

Words to Know

Right Angle:
an angle
that
forms a
square
corner

Obtuse Angle:
an angle greater
than a right angle
but less than a
straight angle

Reflex Angle:
an angle greater
than a
straight
angle

Acute Angle:
an angle
less than
a right angle

Straight Angle:
an angle
formed by a
straight line

209

ON YOUR OWN

1. What types of angles can you find in these signs?

YIELD

STOP

2. Design a traffic sign you think people will notice. Be sure to use at least one of each type of angle.

3. In this piece of stained glass the artist used all types of angles. Design a piece of stained glass using only right angles. Do it again using only acute angles. Then use only obtuse angles. Which do you prefer? Explain your thinking.

4. *My Journal:* What types of angles do you now know about?

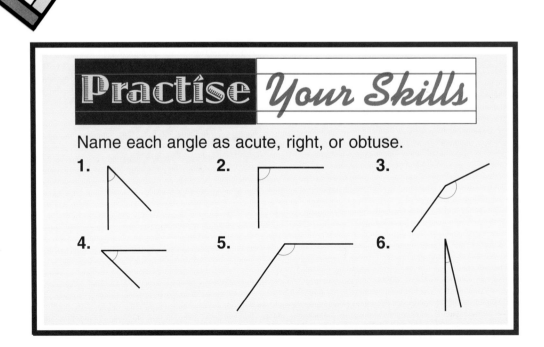

Practise Your Skills

Name each angle as acute, right, or obtuse.

1.

2.

3.

4.

5.

6.

Finding the Measures of Angles

We can measure the sizes of angles using degrees.
The symbol for degrees is °. One complete rotation of a line about a point has a measure of 360°.

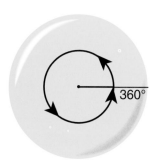

1 Six equilateral triangles meet at a centre point. What is the measure of each angle that touches the centre point? What are the measures of the other angles in each triangle? How do you know?

2 Find the measures of the angles in the Power Polygons.

1. Find a matching angle in these three Power Polygons.
What size is it? Explain your thinking.

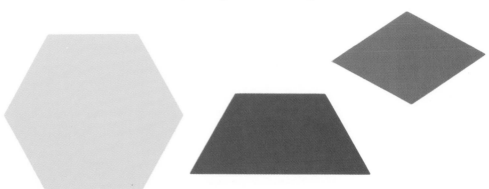

2. Use Power Polygons to make each angle. Find its measure.
Draw a sketch to show what you did. Write
to explain how you know the measure of each angle.

a. Use corners of two Polygons to make an acute angle.

b. Use corners of three Polygons to make a reflex angle.

c. Use corners of three Polygons to make an obtuse angle.

3. *My Journal:* How can you find the measures of angles using
the Power Polygons?

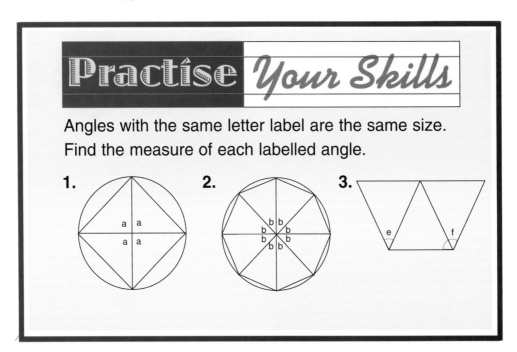

Practise Your Skills

Angles with the same letter label are the same size.
Find the measure of each labelled angle.

1. **2.** **3.**

Using a Protractor

▶ How can you use a protractor to measure angles?

How can you use a protractor to draw angles?

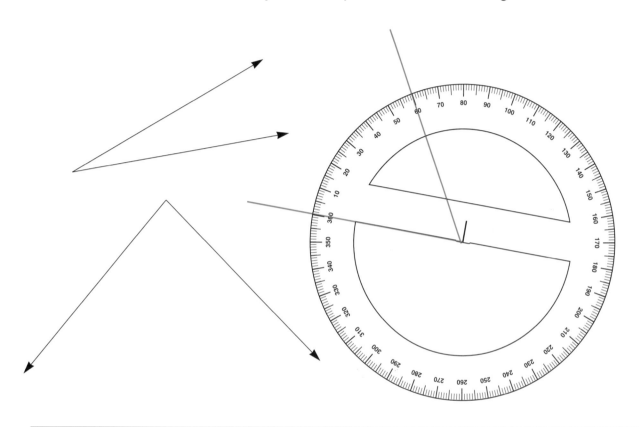

Words to Know

Protractor:
a tool used to measure
the size of an angle

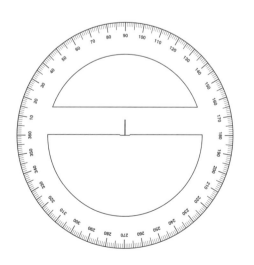

Degree:
the unit of measure used to
measure the size of an angle

ON YOUR OWN

1. What type of angle is shown by the hands on this clock? Draw other hand positions that make the same angle.

2. Draw a pizza that has all of its pieces cut to form angles of about 90°. How many pieces are in it? Draw another pizza with pieces cut at 45° angles. How many pieces are in this pizza? Finally, draw another pizza with pieces cut at 30° angles. Write to describe what you notice.

3. The cover of your book has four right angles. Draw possible book designs in which right angles are not allowed. Write to describe how your designs are different from most book designs.

4. **a.** Draw a triangle that has only one 60° angle. What are the measures of the other angles? What type of triangle is it?

   b. Draw another triangle with only one 60° angle that is different from the one in part a. What are the measures of the other angles? What type of triangle is it?

5. **a.** Draw a polygon. Measure each angle. What is the sum of the angles?

   b. Draw another polygon with the same number of sides as the one in part a. Measure each angle. What is the sum of the angles?

6. *My Journal:* How do you use a protractor to measure angles? How do you use a protractor to draw angles?

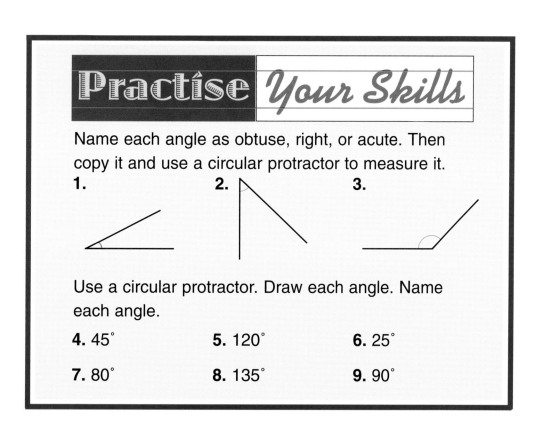

Practise Your Skills

Name each angle as obtuse, right, or acute. Then copy it and use a circular protractor to measure it.

1.   **2.**   **3.**

Use a circular protractor. Draw each angle. Name each angle.

4. 45°   **5.** 120°   **6.** 25°

7. 80°   **8.** 135°   **9.** 90°

Telling Time by the Sky

Today, we take clocks and calendars for granted. It is hard to imagine what our days would be like without them. But how did people tell time before clocks were invented?

For thousands of years, people have observed the changing positions of the sun, moon, and stars. They noticed patterns in the motion of these objects. They used these patterns to measure time.

One of the simplest methods of tracking the sun is to observe the shadow cast by a pole in the ground. Such a pole is called a *gnomon*, or *shadow stick*. It has been used since prehistoric times. The lower the sun is in the sky, the longer the shadow. As the sun rises and sets, the shadow's length changes. The direction of the shadow also changes as the sun appears to move across the sky.

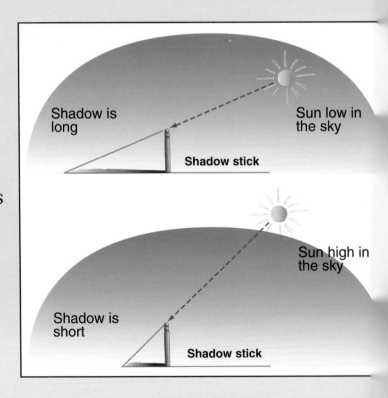

Shadow is long

Sun low in the sky

Shadow stick

Sun high in the sky

Shadow is short

Shadow stick

Some cultures developed more elaborate tools for observing the sky. Almost 4000 years ago, stone-age people built stone circles like the famous Stonehenge. These circles were used to keep track of the rising and setting points of the moon and sun and to predict eclipses.

Astronomers use degrees, not metres, to describe the height of an object above the horizon and the distance between objects in the sky.

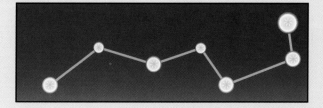

You can use simple hand measures to estimate the height of an object or the distance in degrees between objects. For example, stand with your arm outstretched. Imagine two rays coming out of a point in your shoulder. One ray goes along one side of your little finger. The other goes along the other side of your little finger. The angle these rays make is about a 1° angle.

Sky Measures

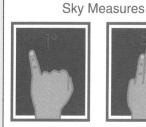

① Use a calendar or newspaper to determine a day when it is a full moon or first-quarter moon. Go outside in the early evening.

② Look for the moon. Use sky measures (hand measures) to estimate its altitude in degrees.

③ Look for the Big Dipper, a group of seven stars arranged as shown above. About how many degrees long is the Big Dipper? About how many degrees wide is the bowl of the Big Dipper?

④ If you know the names of other stars or groups of stars, look for these stars. Use your hand measures to estimate their distances in degrees from the Big Dipper.

MAKING A Hidden-Angle Picture

You have found and described many types of angles. Now it is your turn to create some angles in a picture. Try to hide the angles in the picture.

In your picture, include at least:
- four right angles
- one straight angle
- three obtuse angles, including one of 125°
- three angles whose sum is greater than 180°
- three acute angles, including one of 40°
- three angles whose sum is less than 90°

When you have finished, write a set of clues to help others find your hidden angles.

Check YOURSELF

Great Job! You have created a picture containing all the appropriate angles. Your set of clues tells in a clear way where the hidden angles are located.

MEASURING AND ANALYZING ANGLES

1. Make a copy of the drawing on the right.
On it mark all the right angles you can find.
Use a curved line to mark each angle.

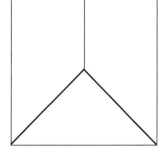

2. Make 4 copies of the drawing in Problem 1.
Use a curved line to mark each of the
following angles.

    a. On the first copy, mark all the reflex angles.

    b. On the second copy, mark all the straight angles.

    c. On the third copy, mark all the acute angles.

    d. On the fourth copy, mark all the obtuse angles.

3. Combine corners of Power Polygons to form these angles.
Trace and label each.

    a. an acute angle   **b.** a 120° angle

    c. a straight angle   **d.** a 180° angle

4. Use combinations of the tan rhombus (Power Polygon O)
and other combinations of Power Polygons.
Find the measures of these angles.

    a. the acute angle
       inside the tan rhombus

    b. the obtuse angle
       inside the tan
       rhombus

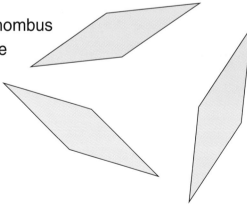

5. LOGO is a computer program for exploring mathematics. You give directions to a turtle to tell it where to move. The turtle draws a path as it moves. LOGO directions tell the turtle how many units to move Forward or Back, and how big an angle to make when it turns Right or Left. For example:

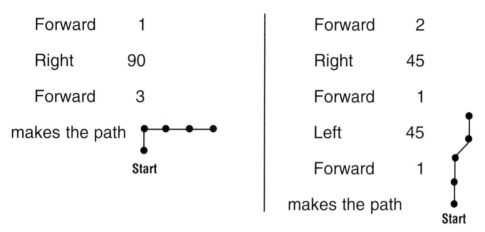

Forward	1		Forward	2
Right	90		Right	45
Forward	3		Forward	1
makes the path			Left	45
			Forward	1
			makes the path	

a. Start at the centre dot. Give LOGO directions for this path.

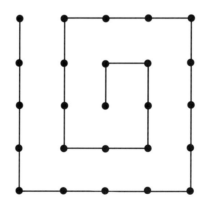

b. Give LOGO directions to make one of your initials.

6. Can a triangle have these angles? Try it.
Explain why or why not. Include a diagram.
  a. an obtuse angle, two acute angles
  b. a 90° angle, a 30° angle, a 60° angle
  c. an obtuse angle, a right angle, an acute angle
  d. two right angles, one acute angle
  e. a 180° angle, a 30° angle, and a 90° angle

S K I L L
BANK
FROM THIS UNIT

1. Is the marked angle a right angle, greater than a right angle, or less than a right angle?

a.  **b.** **c.**

2. Is the marked angle an acute angle, obtuse angle, straight angle, or reflex angle?

a. **b.**   **c.**

3. Find the measure of each labelled angle.

a. 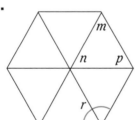 **b.**  **c.**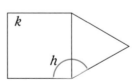

4. Use a circular protractor to measure the angle on the right.

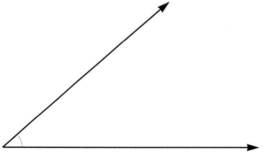

5. Use a circular protractor to draw each angle.
    a. 30°   **b.** 90°   **c.** 110°   **d.** 75°

S K I L L
BANK
LOOKING BACK

The Masses of Ten Children

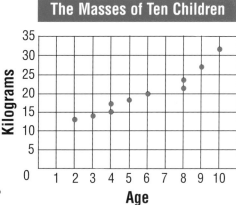

1. Use the scatterplot.

    a. Does it show a relationship between age and mass? Explain how you know.

    b. What do you think the mass of a 7-year-old might be?

2. In four consecutive weeks, Dan jogged 12 km, 15 km, 14 km, and 16 km. Meredith jogged 10 km, 14 km, 18 km, and 20 km. Make a double-bar graph to show the data.

3.

Accidents in May

(histogram: NUMBER OF ACCIDENTS vs TIME: 7-9 AM, 9-11 AM, 11 AM-1 PM, 1-3 PM, 3-5 PM, 5-7 PM)

Examine this histogram. What can you learn about the accidents at this particular intersection?

4. Find each sum or difference.

    a. $\frac{1}{3} + \frac{2}{3}$ **b.** $\frac{1}{2} + \frac{1}{4}$ **c.** $1\frac{1}{8} + \frac{5}{8}$ **d.** $4\frac{1}{6} + 2\frac{1}{3}$

    e. $\frac{3}{4} - \frac{1}{2}$ **f.** $\frac{5}{6} - \frac{1}{3}$ **g.** $5\frac{1}{2} - 1\frac{1}{4}$ **h.** $6\frac{7}{10} - 3\frac{1}{5}$

    i. $4.8 + 16.3$ **j.** $6.2 + 7.34$ **k.** $82.5 - 8.7$ **l.** $67.8 - 9.9$

5. Find each product or quotient.

    a. 5.6×4 **b.** 7.4×7 **c.** 16.3×6

    d. $23.5 \div 5$ **e.** $39.2 \div 4$ **f.** $57.4 \div 7$

6. a. How much is 50% of 80?

    b. How much is 25% of 200?

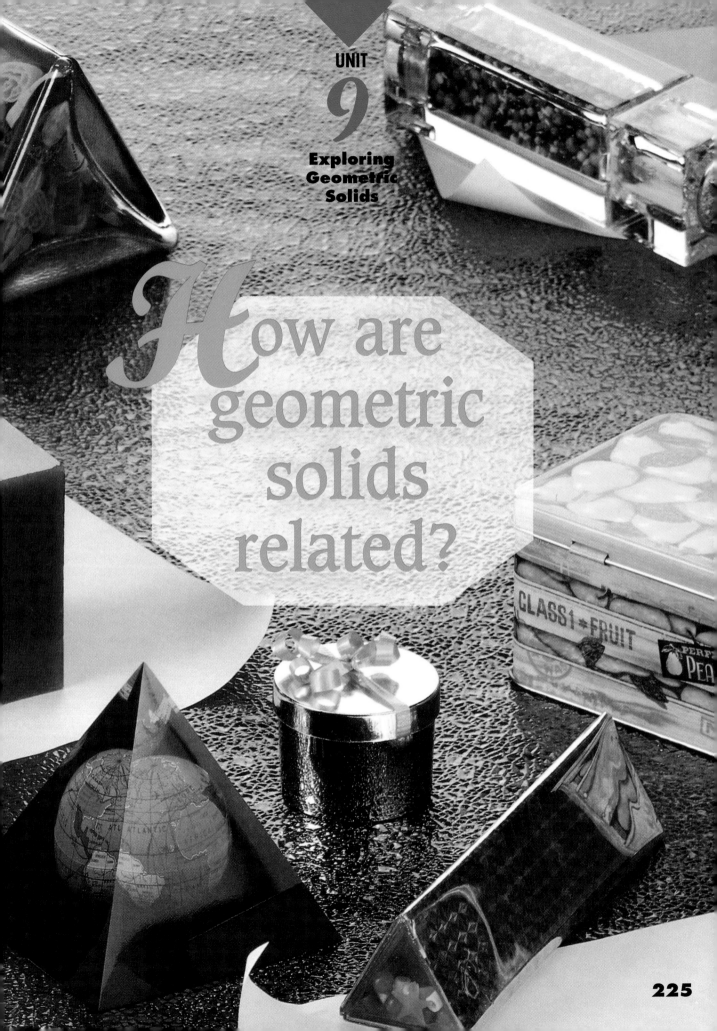

*H*ow are
geometric
solids
related?

EXPLORING GEOMETRIC SOLIDS

S·T·A·R·T·I·N·G OUT

Architect I.M. Pei designed this pyramid
as part of the Louvre museum in Paris.

1. **a.** What figures do you see on one face of the pyramid on page 226?

   b. What is the shape of each face that you see?

   c. What shape do you think the base is?

   d. How many vertices do you think there are in this structure?

Words to Know

Vertex: the point at which edges meet

Face: any flat surface of a solid

Base: the face of a solid on which it stands

Edge: the line of a solid at which two faces meet

My Journal: How are a square and a cube related?
How are a circle and a cylinder related?

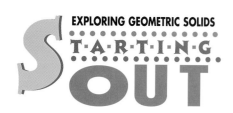

EXPLORING GEOMETRIC SOLIDS

S·T·A·R·T·I·N·G
OUT

2   **a.** Match the three shadows shown to the buildings
     that cast them. Explain your choices.

   b. Draw the shadow you think would be cast by the fourth
     building. Explain your drawing.

Taj Mahal, India

Ontario Place Cinesphere

Calgary Saddledome

Edmonton Space and Science Centre

Words to Know

Octagonal Prism:
a solid in which two congruent, parallel octagons are joined by rectangular faces

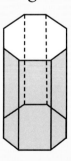

Pentagonal Prism:
a solid in which two congruent, parallel pentagons are joined by rectangular faces

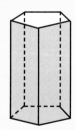

Rectangular Prism:
a solid in which two congruent, parallel rectangles are joined by rectangular faces

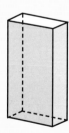

My Journal: Think about the language you use to describe solids. Make a list of the words you find useful.

229

Building Solids

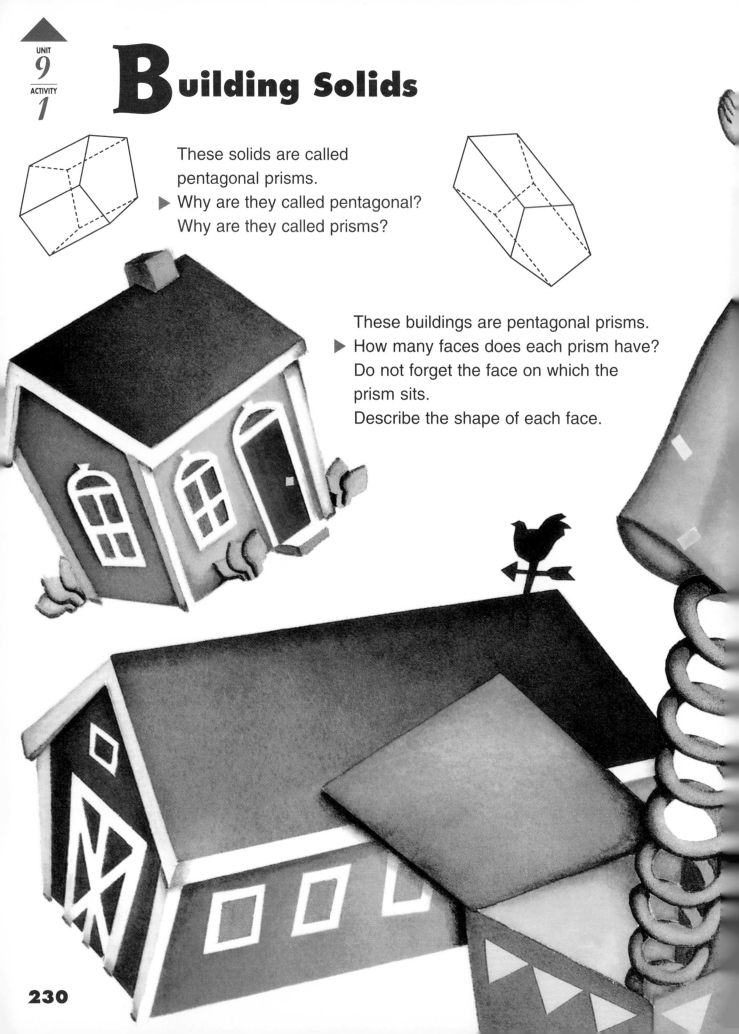

These solids are called pentagonal prisms.

▶ Why are they called pentagonal?
Why are they called prisms?

These buildings are pentagonal prisms.

▶ How many faces does each prism have?
Do not forget the face on which the prism sits.
Describe the shape of each face.

Suppose you cut along 7 edges of a cube. You can unfold it to make a flat pattern or net. This net is called a hexomino. It is made of 6 squares joined at their edges.

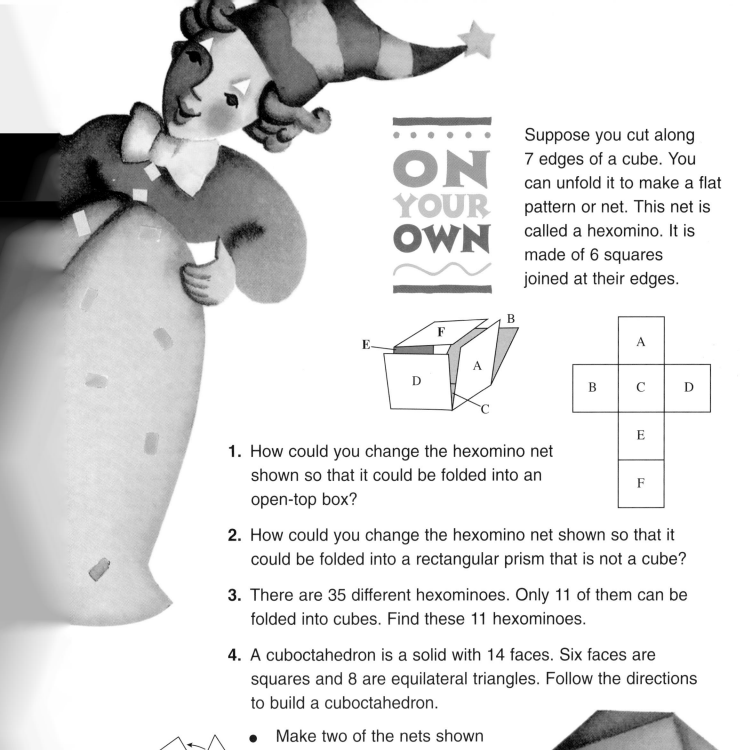

1. How could you change the hexomino net shown so that it could be folded into an open-top box?

2. How could you change the hexomino net shown so that it could be folded into a rectangular prism that is not a cube?

3. There are 35 different hexominoes. Only 11 of them can be folded into cubes. Find these 11 hexominoes.

4. A cuboctahedron is a solid with 14 faces. Six faces are squares and 8 are equilateral triangles. Follow the directions to build a cuboctahedron.

   • Make two of the nets shown on the left. Make your nets much larger.

   • Tape the edges as shown by the arrows. Form a cup-shaped object with each net.

   • Tape the edges of the two cup-shaped objects together.

231

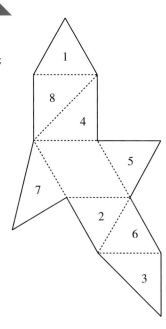

5. Describe the figures in this net.

6. Make a larger copy of the net. Fold along the dotted lines. Tape the net in this order:

- triangle 1 over triangle 2

- triangle 3 over triangle 4

- triangle 5 over triangle 6

- triangle 7 over triangle 8

7. Write a description of the solid you made. Which face would you consider the "bottom"? Why?

8. *My Journal:* Explain how prisms and pyramids are alike and how they are different.

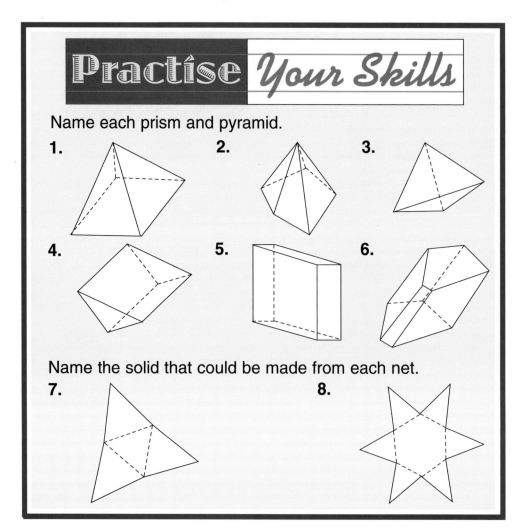

Practise Your Skills

Name each prism and pyramid.

1.   **2.**   **3.**

4.   **5.**   **6.**

Name the solid that could be made from each net.

7.   **8.**

Building Regular Solids

When all the sides of a figure are equal and all the angles are equal, the figure is called *regular*. There are many regular figures.

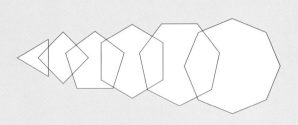
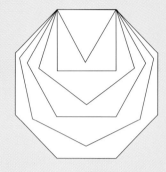

A solid is *regular* when:

- all the faces of the solid are congruent regular polygons
- the same number of faces meet at each vertex
- the same number of edges meet at each vertex

▶ How many regular solids are there?
How can you build them?

One of the regular solids you see frequently is a *cube*.

The chart shows seven types of crystals.

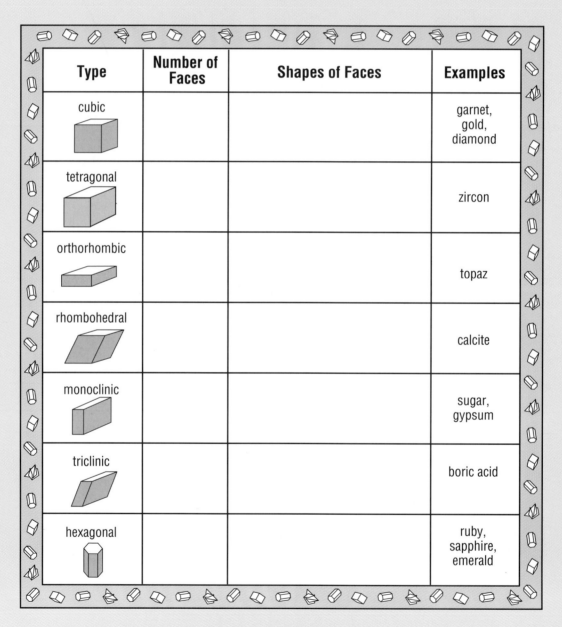

Type	Number of Faces	Shapes of Faces	Examples
cubic			garnet, gold, diamond
tetragonal			zircon
orthorhombic			topaz
rhombohedral			calcite
monoclinic			sugar, gypsum
triclinic			boric acid
hexagonal			ruby, sapphire, emerald

1. Copy the chart. Complete the middle two columns.

2. Which crystal types have all congruent faces? Which are regular solids?

3. This net can be used to make a non-regular solid with all congruent faces. The solid is called a disphenoid. It has faces that are congruent triangles.

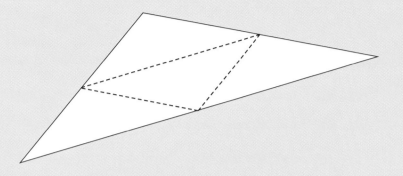

Follow these steps to make a disphenoid.

• Start with any scalene triangle, a triangle in which no two sides are the same length.

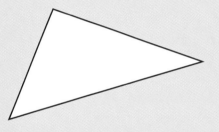

• Use a ruler to find the midpoint of each side. The midpoint of a side divides the side in half.

• Connect the midpoints to make dotted "fold" lines.

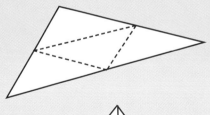

• Fold up to form the solid. Tape its edges.

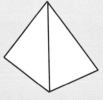

4. Make another disphenoid. This time, start with an isosceles triangle, a triangle with two equal sides. Make the two equal sides each 8 cm. See what happens when you start with an isosceles right triangle, a right triangle with two equal sides.

5. Make two solids made from two copies of this net.
Arrange the solids to form a regular tetrahedron.

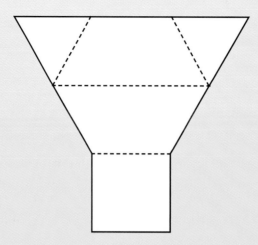

6. *My Journal:* What have you learned about
describing solids?

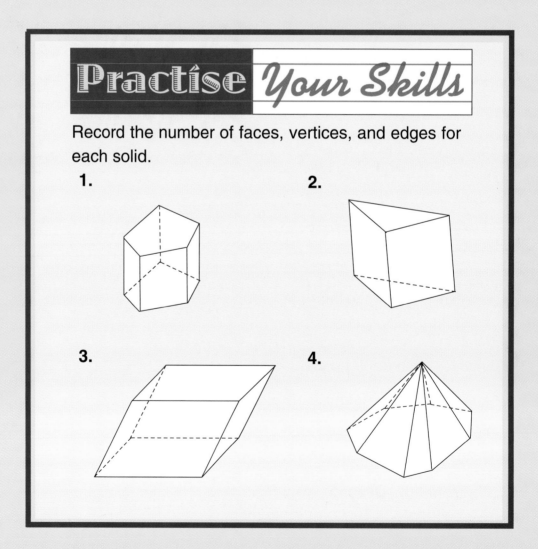

Practise *Your Skills*

Record the number of faces, vertices, and edges for
each solid.

1.

2.

3.

4.

Volume of a Rectangular Prism

▶ Design a box to hold
12 dozen cassette tapes
in their cases.
Label the dimensions
of your box.
Find the volume of your box.

▶ Suppose you wanted your
box to hold double the
number of cassette tapes.
What would you do?

ON
YOUR
OWN

1. Find the volume
of this box.

2. Suppose a
different box
had the same
volume. What
could the
dimensions
of this box be?

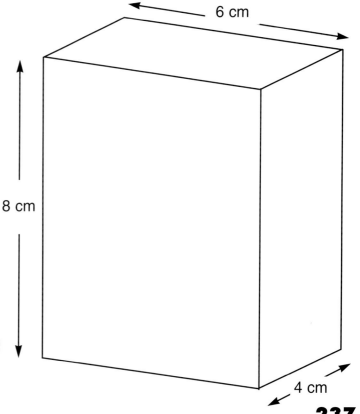

6 cm

8 cm

4 cm

3. Design a box with double the
volume of the box in exercise 1.
Label the dimensions of your box.

4. *My Journal:* Describe how to find
the volume of a rectangular prism.

237

MANUFACTURED
or Natural Containers?

Have you ever wondered what qualities people consider when they want to make a container? Some questions they might ask are: How big does it need to be? How strong? Will it need to be stacked or stored somewhere? What will it contain? What will it be made of?

People frequently build containers with flat surfaces. Most often, the containers they build are boxes with square, rectangular, or other polygonal faces. Why do you think this is so? The materials from which containers are made and storage requirements may affect the shapes of containers.

Nature, on the other hand, rarely has the same requirements. Natural objects often come in containers with non-polygonal shapes. Natural containers are round, curved, or irregularly shaped. Polygonal faces are rare in nature. Some natural containers are shown below.

Recently, excess packaging has become an issue. People have urged companies to cut down on excess packaging for their products.

● ●

1 What ways can you think of to reduce packaging material?

2 How might changing the shape of a package reduce the amount of material required?

3 Why is it important to try to reduce wasteful packaging?

Surface Area

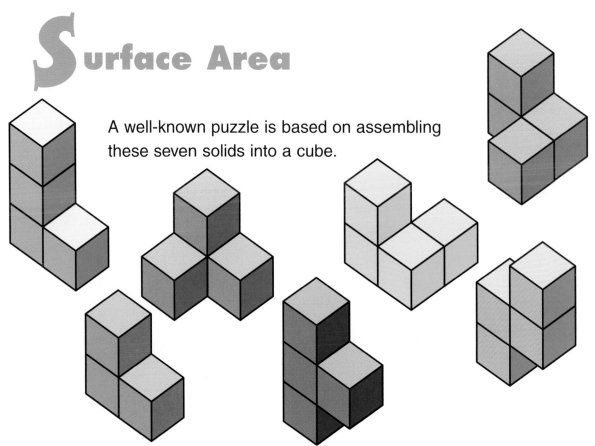

A well-known puzzle is based on assembling these seven solids into a cube.

▶ One solid is made up of three cubes. There is one other way to arrange three cubes. Sketch it. Which arrangement has the greatest surface area? the least surface area?

▶ Six ways to arrange four cubes are shown above. There are two other ways. Sketch them. What is the greatest surface area possible? Which arrangement has the least surface area?

▶ Find the dimensions and volume of the large cube these solids make when connected.

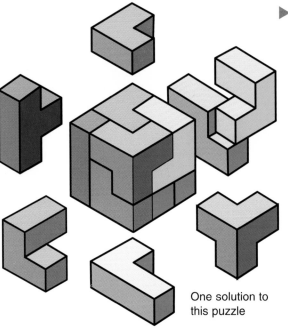

One solution to this puzzle

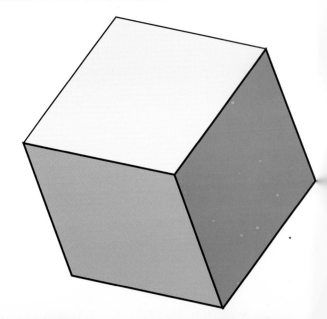

ON YOUR OWN

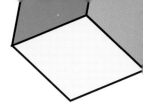

▶ Find all the rectangular prisms you can build with each number of cubes. For each number of cubes, which rectangular prism has the least surface area? the greatest surface area?

1. 8 cubes

2. 27 cubes

3. 36 cubes

4. 48 cubes

5. 60 cubes

6. *My Journal*: What have you learned about the relationship between volume and surface area?

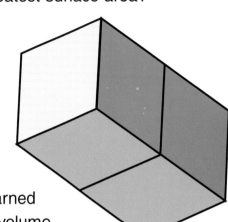

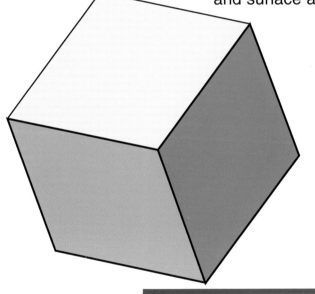

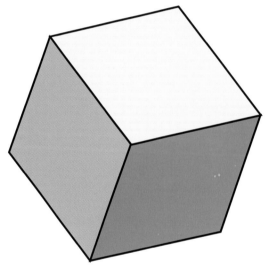

Practise Your Skills

Copy and complete the chart for rectangular prisms.

Length	Width	Height	Volume	Surface Area
4 cm	2 cm	5 cm	?	?
4 cm	2 cm	10 cm	?	?
4 cm	4 cm	5 cm	?	?
8 cm	2 cm	5 cm	?	?
?	?	?	160 cm³	?

It's the Age of Aquariums!

Fish need oxygen to live. The amount of oxygen in the tank depends more on the area of the water surface than on the volume of water. An aquarium fish longer than 8 cm needs about 60 cm² of water surface for every 1 cm of body length. A tropical fish under 8 cm needs only 50 cm² to 65 cm² of water surface.

Some Possible Dimensions for
Tropical Fish Aquariums

Length x Width x Height (centimetres)

20 x 15 x 15
30 x 15 x 15
35 x 20 x 20
45 x 25 x 25
60 x 30 x 30
75 x 30 x 40
90 x 30 x 40
120 x 40 x 40

Choose your own!

- Design your own aquarium. Choose the fish you want. Then decide on the size aquarium you need.
- Find the water capacity in litres of your aquarium. Use 1000 cm³ = 1 L.
- Suppose you built the tank. Find the area of the glass you would need.

Tropical Fish Lengths

Name	Length (cm)
black mollie	7.5
glow-light tetra	4.0
paradise fish	7.5
guppy	2.5
zebra fish	5.0
neon tetra	4.0
beacon fish	4.5

Name	Length (cm)
Malayan loach	10.0
red platy	4.0
blue gourami	10.0
catfish	6.5
swordtail	8.2
ruby barb	6.5
angel fish	13.0

CheckYOURSELF

Great Job! Your aquarium is big enough for the fish you chose. You found its capacity and the area of the glass needed. You wrote to explain how you used volume and surface area in your plans.

EXPLORING GEOMETRIC SOLIDS

PROBLEM BANK

1. Which of these hexominoes can be folded into a cube? Explain how you know.

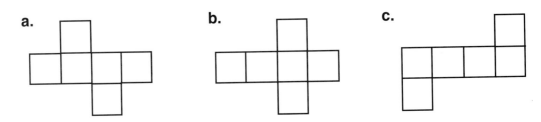

a.

b.

c.

2. a. This is a hexagonal prism. What is the shape of the slice shown? How do you know?

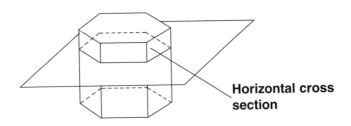

Horizontal cross section

b. Draw each solid with its base horizontal. Describe the shape of the horizontal cross section of each solid.

- rectangular prism
- triangular prism
- cylinder
- cone

c. Does the shape or size of the horizontal cross section depend upon how high or low the slice is made? Explain.

d. Describe the shapes of the *vertical* cross sections of the hexagonal prism.

3. These cubes were made by stacking 2, 3, and 4 centimetre cubes along each edge.

2 cm

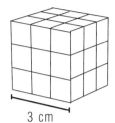

3 cm

4 cm

a. Make a T-table. Show the volumes of cubes with edges that are 2 cm, 3 cm, 4 cm, 5 cm, and 6 cm in length.

b. Draw a graph. Use the ordered pairs from your T-table. Describe your graph.

Edge Length (in cm)	Volume (in cm³)
2	8
3	?
4	?
5	?
6	?

4. a. Make a T-table. Show the surface areas of cubes with edges that are 2 cm, 3 cm, 4 cm, 5 cm, and 6 cm in length.

b. Draw a graph. Use the ordered pairs from your T-table. Describe your graph.

Edge Length (in cm)	Surface Area (in cm²)
2	24
3	?
4	?
5	?
6	?

SKILL BANK FROM THIS UNIT

1. Name each solid.

a. 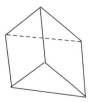 **b.** 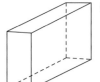 **c.** 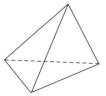 **d.**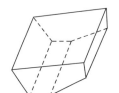

2. Name the solid that could be made from each net.

a.

b.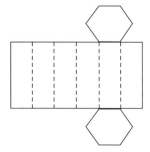

3. Sketch a net for each solid.

a.   **b.** 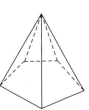 **c.**   **d.**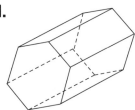

4. Find the surface area of each rectangular prism.

a.  **b.** 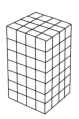 **c.** 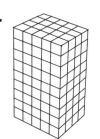 **d.**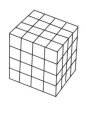

5. Find the volume of each rectangular prism in problem 4.

SKILL BANK

LOOKING BACK

1. Find each sum or difference.

    a. $\frac{1}{4} + \frac{3}{4}$ **b.** $\frac{1}{2} + \frac{1}{3}$ **c.** $1\frac{3}{8} + 7\frac{1}{8}$ **d.** $3\frac{1}{6} + 1\frac{1}{2}$

    e. $\frac{4}{5} - \frac{1}{5}$ **f.** $\frac{1}{2} - \frac{1}{4}$ **g.** $6\frac{7}{10} - 2\frac{3}{10}$ **h.** $3\frac{5}{8} - \frac{1}{2}$

    i. $34.8 + 6.3$ **j.** $97.4 - 18.26$ **k.** $48.21 - 2.9$ **l.** $10.7 + 38.9$

2. Find each product or quotient.

    a. 55.6×3 **b.** 14.3×8 **c.** 67.4×7

    d. $42.5 \div 5$ **e.** $30.4 \div 4$ **f.** $73.8 \div 6$

3. Give your answer first as a fraction, then as a percent.

    a. 400 in all: what part is 100?   **b.** 200 in all: what part is 50?

    c. 50 in all: what part is 40?

4. Name each angle.

    a.   **b.**   **c.**

5. What is the measure of each labelled angle?

    a.    **b.**

6. Copy each angle and extend the rays.
Use a circular protractor. Measure each angle.

    a. 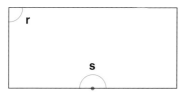   **b.**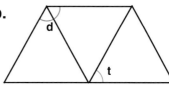

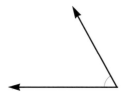
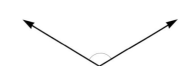

What is the chance an outcome will occur?

1 Explain what the words *chance*, *outcome*, and *likely* mean to each person here.

My Journal: When do you think about what is likely or not likely to happen? How do you predict what you think will happen?

LINE UP CARDS

Offence
Kenny Chan
Mark Goode
Jennie Franklin
Defence
Sam Rajnathan
Maria Rodrigues

TEAM LIST
JETS 1994-1995 (Team 1)

Ahmed, Faraz	D
Brown, Timothy	LW
Chan, Kenny	C
Chang, Hsiao	RW
Franklin, Jennie	LW
Goode, Mark	RW
Grossi, Paola	C
Rajnathan, Sam	D
Roberts, Cherie	D
Rodrigues, Maria	D
Sherman, Janelle	RW
Sheth, Farah	D
Stern, Alison	C
White, Winston	D
Yip, Jimmy	LW

Offence
Paolo Grossi
Hsiao Chang
Timothy Brown
Defence
Winston White
Farah Sheth

Offence
Alison Stern
Janelle Sherman
Jimmy Yip
Defence
Cherie Roberts
Faraz Ahmed

2 **a.** What information about the players can you tell from the team list? How has this information been used to create the lineup cards?

b. Do you think you could have made other combinations? Explain.

c. What do you notice about the game schedule?

d. Do you think there could have been other combinations? Explain.

e. What different ways might you expect to see the player dressed to play hockey?

My Journal: What other situations with many combinations can you think of?

Schedule of Fall Games				
Week 1	Week 2	Week 3	Week 4	Week 5
1 v. 6	1 v. 5	1 v. 4	1 v. 2	1 v. 3
2 v. 5	2 v. 4	2 v. 3	3 v. 5	2 v. 6
3 v. 4	3 v. 6	5 v. 6	4 v. 6	4 v. 5

Teams:
1. Jets
2. Stars
3. Comets
4. Lions
5. Bruins
6. Tigers

Experimental Probability

1 Suppose you toss a coin.
How can it land?

2 Is one outcome more likely than the other?

1. Suppose you tossed a coin 50 times. How many times do you think it will land heads?

2. Try it. Toss a coin 50 times. Keep a tally of the results.

3. What fraction of the 50 tosses landed heads? What fraction of the 50 tosses landed tails?

4. Was your prediction close?

5. Compare your results with the results of other students. Did all of you get the same results?

6. Combine your tally with someone else's. What fraction of the tosses landed heads?

7. *My Journal:* In a probability experiment, you should make many tries. Explain why.

Practise Your Skills

Copy and complete to write equivalent fractions.

1. $\frac{1}{2} = \frac{2}{4} = \frac{3}{6} = \frac{4}{8} = \frac{\blacksquare}{\blacksquare} = \frac{\blacksquare}{\blacksquare} = \frac{\blacksquare}{\blacksquare} = \frac{\blacksquare}{\blacksquare}$

2. $\frac{3}{10} = \frac{6}{20} = \frac{9}{30} = \frac{\blacksquare}{\blacksquare} = \frac{\blacksquare}{\blacksquare} = \frac{\blacksquare}{\blacksquare}$

3. $\frac{3}{4} = \frac{6}{8} = \frac{9}{12} = \frac{\blacksquare}{\blacksquare} = \frac{\blacksquare}{\blacksquare} = \frac{\blacksquare}{\blacksquare} = \frac{\blacksquare}{\blacksquare} = \frac{\blacksquare}{\blacksquare}$

Theoretical Probability

▶ Construct a cube from a net.
Choose any numbers from 1 to 6.
You may repeat some numbers.
You may omit some numbers.
What is the probability of
rolling each number
on your cube?

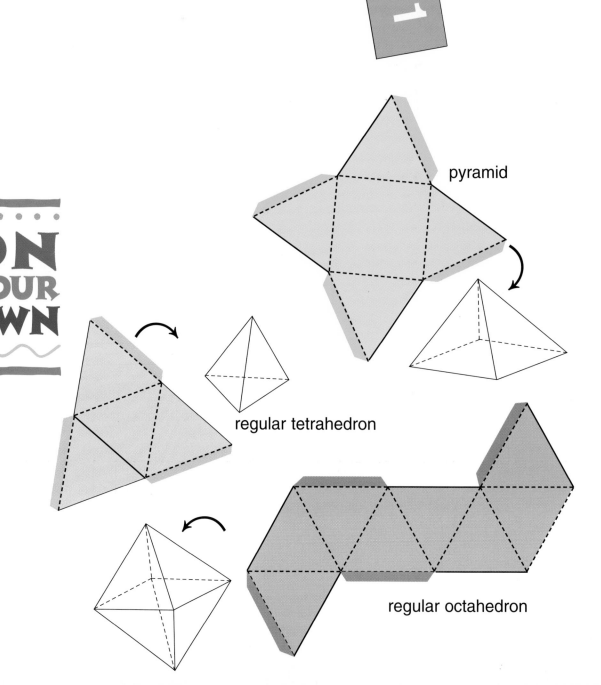

pyramid

regular tetrahedron

regular octahedron

ON YOUR OWN

1. **a.** Use a net to construct a regular tetrahedron and a regular octahedron, as shown on page 256. Colour or mark each face as described below.
   - the regular tetrahedron: red, red, blue, yellow
   - the regular octahedron: X, X, X, O, O, O, O, O

   b. Suppose you rolled each solid. List the possible outcomes. Calculate the probability of each outcome.

   c. Suppose you were to roll each solid 40 times. How many times could you expect each outcome to occur?

   d. Roll each solid 40 times. Record the outcomes. How close were your experimental results to your calculated results?

2. Use a net to make a pyramid. Notice that the faces do not all have the same shape. Will all the faces have an equal chance of being rolled? Test it out by rolling the solid 50 times. Write about what you found.

3. *My Journal:* Describe how to find the probability of an outcome.

Practise Your Skills

Find the probability of each colour landing face down when the solid is rolled.

1. 4 congruent faces; 1 face is red

2. 6 congruent faces; all 6 faces are blue

3. 8 congruent faces; 6 faces are green, 2 are white

4. 12 congruent faces; 3 faces are red, 8 are blue, and 1 is yellow

Connecting Probabilities with Outcomes

1, 1, 3, 3, 5, 6

1, 2, 3, 4, 5, 6

4, 1, 1, 3, 2, 5, 5, 3

6, 4, 3, 2, 1, 1

2, 3, 3, 4, 6, 6

2, 2, 3, 2, 3

2, 1, 2, 3, 2, 2, 4, 2

Match each probability to a solid on page 258.

a. The probability of rolling a 2 is $\frac{5}{8}$.

b. The probability of rolling an odd number is the same as the probability of rolling an even number.

c. The probability of rolling an odd number is $\frac{5}{6}$.

d. The probability of rolling a number greater than 3 is $\frac{1}{2}$.

e. The probability of rolling a 1 is $\frac{1}{6}$.

f. The probability of rolling a prime number is 1.

g. The probability of rolling an even number is $\frac{1}{4}$.

 The probability of rolling a 1 on a particular tetrahedron is $\frac{1}{4}$. The other faces may have any of the numbers 1, 2, 3, or 4. How could the tetrahedron be numbered? Write as many different ways as you can.

1. a. Design two different spinners, each with the probability of $\frac{1}{5}$ of spinning a 2.

b. Design two different spinners, each with the probability of $\frac{3}{4}$ of spinning a number less than 6

2. *My Journal:* What have you learned about probability by using solids?

Using Probability to Predict Results

Suppose you looked at all the telephone numbers in a book. Suppose you added the last two digits of a telephone number.

▶ What sums are possible? Make a number line with the possible sums.

- Above the number line, plot an X for each way to get a sum of 0.
- Plot an X for each way to get a sum of 1.
- Keep on in this way until you have plotted an X for each way to get each of the sums.

1 How many pieces of data did you plot in all?

2 How many different ways can you get a sum of 9? What is the probability of getting a sum of 9?

3 What is the probability of getting each of the other sums?

1. A cube is labelled 1, 1, 2, 2, 3, and 3.

Suppose you roll
it 36 times.
How often would
you expect to roll a 2?

2.

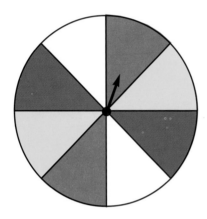

Suppose you spin this
spinner 40 times. How many
times would you expect to
spin red?

3. Two cubes are each labelled 1, 2, 3, 4, 5, and 6. Suppose you roll them
36 times. How many times would you expect their sum to be at least 10?

4. Suppose you spin these spinners
48 times and multiply the numbers
spun each time. How many times
would you expect to get a product
that is an even number?

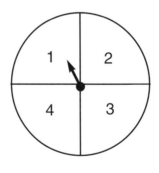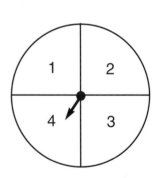

5. *My Journal:* How can you use
probability to predict events?

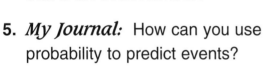

Copy and complete each pair of equivalent fractions.

1. $\frac{1}{6} = \frac{?}{36}$ **2.** $\frac{1}{8} = \frac{?}{48}$ **3.** $\frac{1}{3} = \frac{?}{60}$ **4.** $\frac{1}{5} = \frac{?}{50}$

5. $\frac{3}{4} = \frac{?}{60}$ **6.** $\frac{2}{3} = \frac{?}{48}$ **7.** $\frac{3}{8} = \frac{?}{48}$ **8.** $\frac{2}{5} = \frac{?}{40}$

TAKING Chances

Dreidel is a game usually played during the Jewish holiday of Hannukah. Each of the four sides of the dreidel has one of the Hebrew letters nun, gimel, heh, or shin. Each player has 10 counters and puts two of them in the middle to form a pot. Then players take turns spinning the dreidel. If the dreidel lands on nun, the player takes no counters from the pot.

If it lands on heh, the player takes half the counters from the pot. If it lands on gimel, the player takes the whole pot. If it lands on the unlucky shin, however, the player must add a counter to the pot.

1 What are the chances of the dreidel landing on each of the four sides? How do you know?

Shin　Heh　Gimel　Nun

2 Would the chances be different if the dreidel had 8 sides, with each letter on 2 of them? What if it had 16 sides with each letter on 4 of them?

3 Try playing Dreidel with friends. How many times did you land on gimel? Do you think that this game involves mostly chance or skill?

Finding Probabilities for Combinations

Mix-and-Match Clothes has introduced a new line of clothing. There are 4 different shirts, 3 different pairs of pants, and 3 different sweaters. The manager has decided to display a different outfit in the front window each week.

1 How many different outfits are possible?

2 Look at the mannequin on the left on page 265. What is the probability that the first week's outfit will be worn by that mannequin?

1. What is the probability that the first week's outfit will include each item?

   a. tan shirt

   b. brown pants

   c. white shirt and black pants

   d. brown pants and green sweater

   e. grey shirt and green sweater

   f. red sweater

   g. blue shirt, black pants, and tan sweater

   h. a shirt

2. *My Journal:* How can you find all the possible outcomes for combinations of things?

Fishing for the Answer

How many ways can a fish sandwich be ordered?

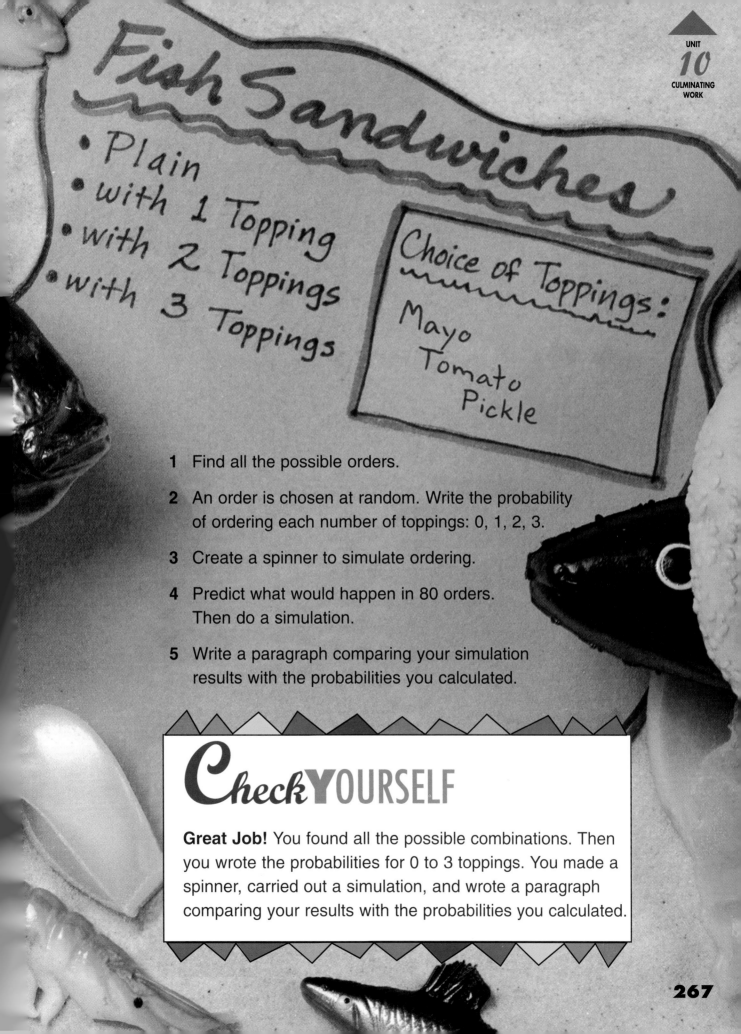

Fish Sandwiches

- Plain
- with 1 Topping
- with 2 Toppings
- with 3 Toppings

Choice of Toppings:

Mayo
Tomato
Pickle

1 Find all the possible orders.

2 An order is chosen at random. Write the probability of ordering each number of toppings: 0, 1, 2, 3.

3 Create a spinner to simulate ordering.

4 Predict what would happen in 80 orders. Then do a simulation.

5 Write a paragraph comparing your simulation results with the probabilities you calculated.

Check YOURSELF

Great Job! You found all the possible combinations. Then you wrote the probabilities for 0 to 3 toppings. You made a spinner, carried out a simulation, and wrote a paragraph comparing your results with the probabilities you calculated.

P R O B L E M
BANK

1. Take a place marker from a game or a small piece from a construction set such as Lego®. Decide how many different ways it can land when you roll it. Predict how often it will land each way. Express your predictions as fractions and record them. Then test it out. Decide how many times you should roll the object. Do the experiment, recording each roll. Compare the results with your predictions. Write a report of your experiment.

2. A deck of playing cards has 52 cards. It is made up of 4 suits: spades, hearts, diamonds, and clubs. Spades and clubs are black cards. Hearts and diamonds are red cards. Each suit is made up of 13 cards: 2, 3, 4, 5, 6, 7, 8, 9, 10, jack, queen, king, and ace. The jack, queen, and king are called face cards.

Suppose you draw a card from a shuffled deck. What is the probability of each outcome?

a. a spade   **b.** a red card

c. a queen   **d.** a 4

e. a face card   **f.** a 15

g. a number from 2 to 10

3. Karin is designing a game that uses two number cubes. One cube is white and the other yellow. She can number them using any of the numbers from 1 to 6. Players will be able to choose which of the two cubes they wish to roll. How can Karin number the cubes to have these probabilities?

  a. The probability of rolling a 6 with the white cube is $\frac{1}{6}$. The probability of rolling an even number with the yellow cube is $\frac{5}{6}$.

  b. The probability of rolling a 1 with the white cube is $\frac{1}{2}$. The probability of rolling a number less than 4 with the yellow cube is $\frac{2}{3}$.

4. • Play with a partner. Each of you needs 16 counters and a large 4-by-4 grid. You also need two number cubes labelled 1 to 6. Fill in your grid with any of the numbers from 0 to 5.

  • When it is your turn, roll the number cubes. Subtract the lesser number from the greater. Place a counter on that number on your grid. The winner is the first player to get four counters in a row or column. If no player does, the one who covers the grid first wins.

  • Write to explain the strategies you can use to win.

5. An ice cream store has a 99¢ sale with several choices.

    cone: sugar or plain
    one scoop: ice cream, sherbet, or yogurt
    one topping: chocolate, nuts, or sprinkles

Suppose all the choices are so popular that they are equally likely. What is the probability of each choice?

  a. a sugar cone   **b.** sherbet
  c. nuts   **d.** ice cream with sprinkles
  e. a plain cone with yogurt and nuts

SKILL BANK
FROM THIS UNIT

1. Copy and complete each pair of equivalent fractions.

a. $\frac{1}{3} = \frac{\blacksquare}{60}$ **b.** $\frac{1}{4} = \frac{\blacksquare}{36}$ **c.** $\frac{1}{2} = \frac{\blacksquare}{100}$ **d.** $\frac{5}{8} = \frac{\blacksquare}{80}$

e. $\frac{2}{3} = \frac{\blacksquare}{60}$ **f.** $\frac{4}{4} = \frac{\blacksquare}{48}$ **g.** $\frac{4}{5} = \frac{\blacksquare}{50}$ **h.** $\frac{6}{6} = \frac{\blacksquare}{60}$

2. This is the tally for some spins of a spinner.

red	卌 卌 卌 卌 卌 卌 卌 I
blue	卌 卌 卌 卌 IIII

What fraction of the spins landed on red?
What fraction landed on blue?

3. Three solids are listed below. Three faces of each solid are marked with an A. The other faces are labelled with other letters. Find the probability of rolling an A for each solid.

a. a regular tetrahedron   **b.** a cube   **c.** a regular octahedron

4. What is the probability of spinning red for each spinner?

a. 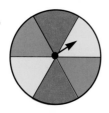   **b.** 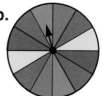   **c.**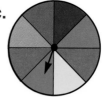

5. Write a set of numbers for the faces of each cube.

a. The probability of rolling a 1 is $\frac{1}{2}$.
b. The probability of rolling an odd number is $\frac{2}{3}$.

6. 3 styles, 5 fabrics, 3 colours.
How many combinations are possible?
What is the probability of any one of them?

S K I L L BANK
LOOKING BACK

1. Name each angle.

a.

b.

c.

2. What are the measures of the angles in an equilateral triangle?

3. What is the measure of an angle that makes a square corner?

4. Use a circular protractor. Draw each angle.
   a. 45°   **b.** 150°   **c.** 15°   **d.** 80°

5. Identify each solid.

a. 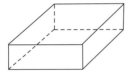   **b.** 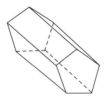   **c.**

d. 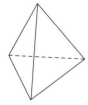   **e.**   **f.**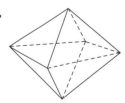

6. Look at the solids in problem 5. How many vertices does each have?

7. What is the volume of this box?

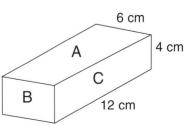

8. Use the box in problem 7. Find each area.
   a. face A   **b.** face B
   c. face C   **d.** all the faces

*H*ow can we
measure area
and perimeter?

Name

*C*entimetre Gr

MEASURING AREA
AND PERIMETER

S·T·A·R·T·I·N·G
OUT

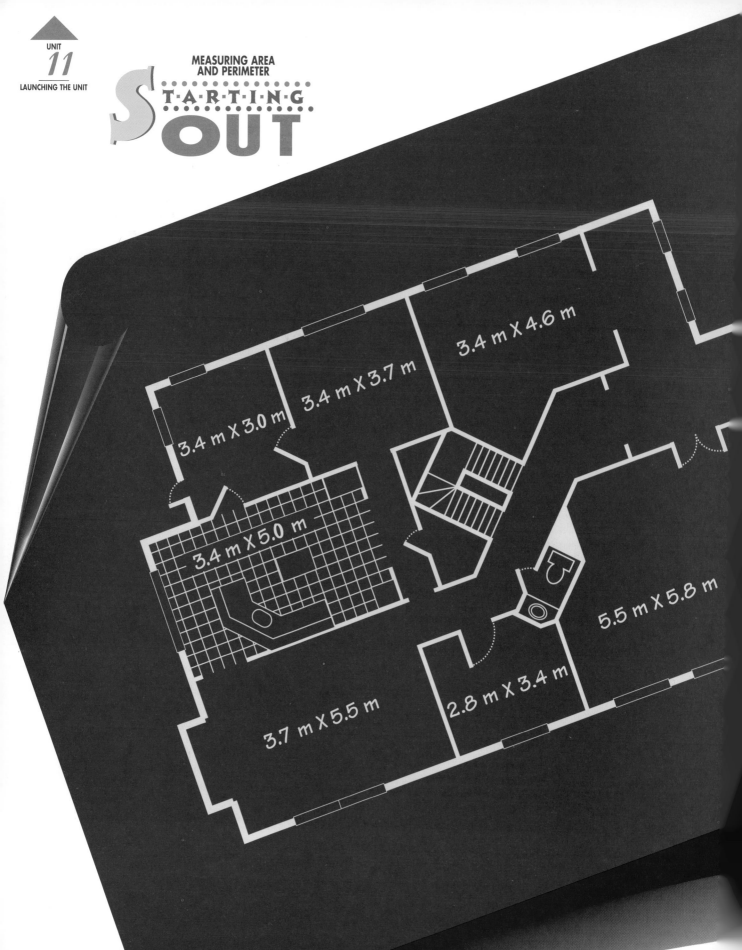

3.4 m X 3.0 m

3.4 m X 3.7 m

3.4 m X 4.6 m

3.4 m X 5.0 m

5.5 m X 5.8 m

3.7 m X 5.5 m

2.8 m X 3.4 m

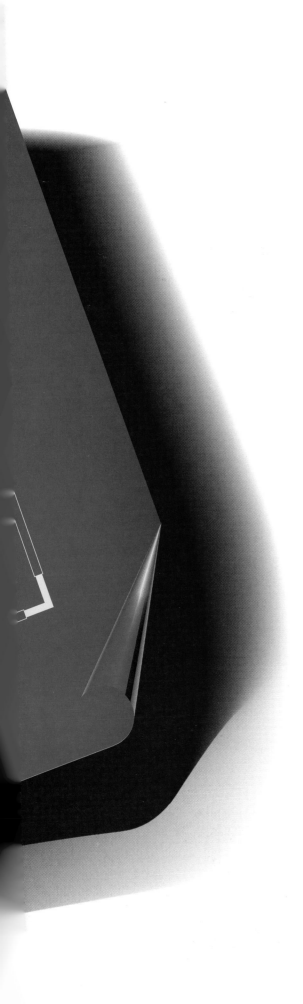

1 **a.** How would you find the floor area of each room?

b. How would you find the total floor area of the apartment?

c. How would you find the perimeter of each room?

d. When might you need to know the area of a room?

e. When might you need to know the perimeter of a room?

My Journal: What do you know about measuring area and perimeter? How do you think area and perimeter are related?

Words to Know
Area: the amount of space a figure covers **Perimeter:** the distance around a figure **Polygon:** a closed figure with straight sides

Finding Perimeter

Karen and Alberto jog 5 km each day after school.
The basketball court in their school gym is 26 m long
and 14 m wide.

▶ How many times will they have to jog around the outside
lines of the basketball court each day to jog 5 km?

▶ Find the perimeter of each figure without adding all the
side lengths. Write to explain your strategies.

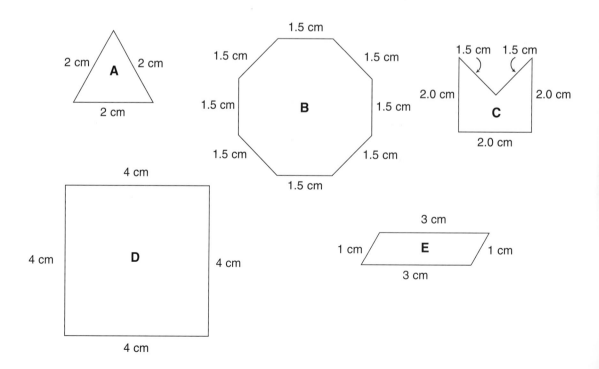

ON YOUR OWN

1. Draw a polygon for which you need to measure the length of only one side to find the perimeter.

2. Draw a polygon for which you need to measure the lengths of two sides to find the perimeter.

3. Draw a polygon for which you need to measure the lengths of all sides to find the perimeter.

4. *My Journal:* What have you learned about finding the perimeters of polygons?

Practise Your Skills

1. Find the perimeter of each figure.

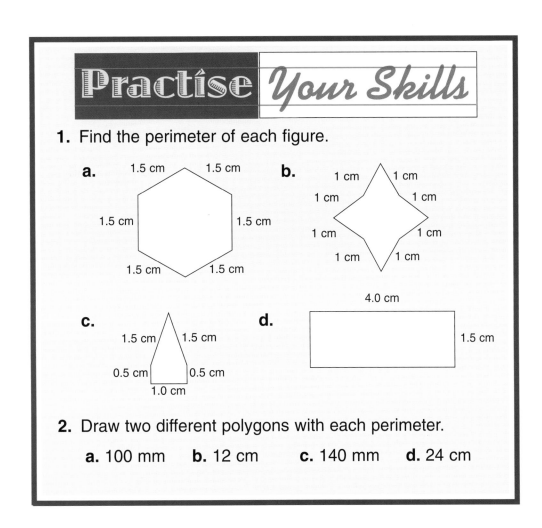

a.
1.5 cm   1.5 cm
1.5 cm   1.5 cm
1.5 cm   1.5 cm

b.
1 cm   1 cm
1 cm   1 cm
1 cm   1 cm
1 cm   1 cm

c.
1.5 cm   1.5 cm
0.5 cm   0.5 cm
1.0 cm

d.
4.0 cm
1.5 cm

2. Draw two different polygons with each perimeter.

   a. 100 mm   b. 12 cm   c. 140 mm   d. 24 cm

Area of a Rectangle

Suppose you build a deck around a rectangular swimming pool. The deck is 2 m wide. The pool is 6 m wide and 12 m long.

▶ What is the area of the deck?

▶ Suppose you choose square patio tiles that are 50 cm on each side to build the deck. How many tiles will you need? Suppose each tile costs $4.95. How much will the tiles cost?

1. Follow these steps to make a parallelogram from a rectangle.

Step 1
Draw and cut out a 15 cm by 6 cm rectangle.

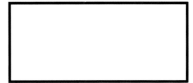

Step 2
Cut off a triangle starting at a vertex.

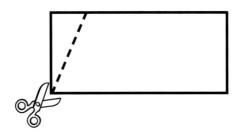

Step 3
Tape the triangle to the opposite side.

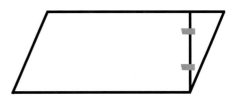

2. What was the area of the rectangle before you cut off the triangle?

What is the area of the parallelogram? How do you know?

3. Draw a diagonal line to divide the parallelogram into two congruent triangles.

What is the area of each triangle? Explain how you know.

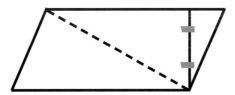

4. *My Journal:* How does knowing how to find the area of a rectangle help you to find the areas of a parallelogram and a triangle?

Practise Your Skills

Find the area of each rectangle.

1.

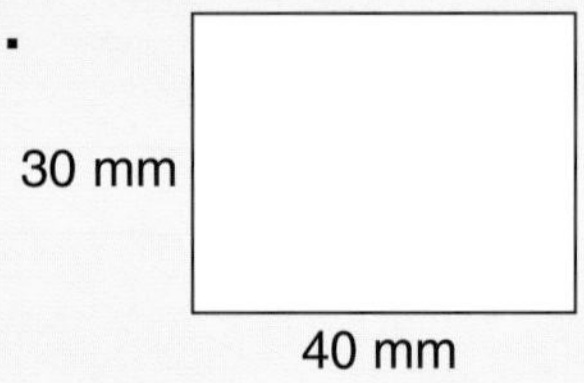

30 mm

40 mm

2.

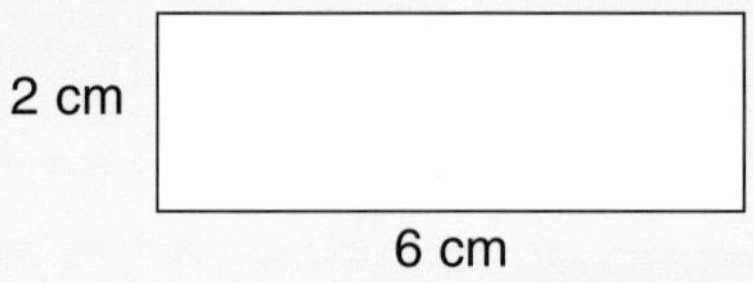

2 cm

6 cm

3.

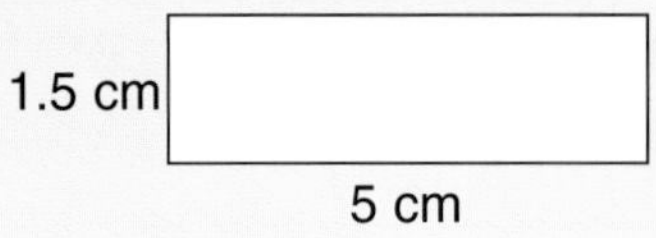

1.5 cm

5 cm

4.

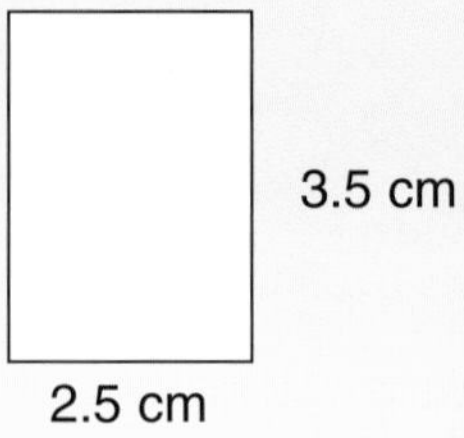

3.5 cm

2.5 cm

Draw two different rectangles with each area.

5. 16 cm²   **6.** 150 mm²   **7.** 24 cm²   **8.** 120 mm²

Relating Area and Perimeter

Each square table seats one person on each side. Thirty-six square tables can be pushed together to form a large rectangular banquet table.

▶ How many arrangements can you make?

▶ Which arrangement will seat the greatest number of people?

ON YOUR OWN

1. A teacher assigned this problem:

Trace one shoe on a copy of 1-cm grid paper.

Then use any method to find the approximate area of your shoe.

This is the method Samuel reported:

This is how I found the area of my shoe.

I placed string around the outline of my shoe.

I cut a piece of string equal to the perimeter.

I arranged the string in the shape of a rectangle on 1-cm Grid Paper and figured out its area. This way, I did not have to count squares and part squares.

Investigate Samuel's method of finding the area of his shoe.

Write to describe your conclusions.

2. The area of a rectangle is 36 mm². Find the greatest whole-number perimeter the rectangle could have.

3. Suppose you have to build a run in your backyard for your dog. The run is rectangular. You have 40 m of fencing and want to use all of it. Draw two possible runs that you could build. Which run would be better? Explain.

4. A certain brand of garden fencing is sold in cartons of 60 sections. Each section is 0.5 m long.
   a. Suppose you bought one carton of fencing. What is the area of the largest rectangular garden you can fence?
   b. Suppose you want to fence a rectangular garden with an area of 100 m². What is the least number of cartons of fencing you would need to buy?

5. *My Journal:* What have you learned about the relationship between area and perimeter?

Practise *Your Skills*

Draw a rectangle with the greatest perimeter for each area. Use side lengths that are whole numbers.

1. 30 cm²   **2.** 18 cm²   **3.** 15 cm²   **4.** 360 mm²

Draw a rectangle with the least area for each perimeter. Use side lengths that are whole numbers.

5. 14 cm   **6.** 260 mm   **7.** 20 cm   **8.** 30 cm

Draw a square with each perimeter. What is the area of the square? Then draw a rectangle with the same area.

9. 40 cm   **10.** 32 cm   **11.** 56 cm   **12.** 24 cm

MEASURING OUR WORLD

Since prehistoric times, people have sought ways to measure and describe the world around them.

It is useless to have a unit of measure if no one else knows what it means. So, early measures were based on the lengths of parts of the human body. By using the lengths of body parts, everyone had her or his own "built-in" measurements. There were some problems with this — not everyone has the same size arm, foot, or hand! But even if your hand might not exactly match someone else's, you could still use it to get a sense of the size of an object.

These measurements were standardized within a country or region. The official length of a foot, for example, might be set to equal the measurement of the king's or chief's foot. An object with this length would be crafted from stone or metal and kept in a safe place. All other measurements would be compared to it. Its length could be marked on sticks or ropes for other people to use.

The Babylonians, Egyptians, Hebrews, Greeks, and Romans used the distance from the elbow to the tip of the middle finger as a unit of measure. This measure was called a *cubit*.

Work with a partner. Answer these questions to investigate early systems of measurement. You will need a ruler, a measuring tape, and some string.

1 Because measures were based on adult body lengths, you will need to gather data from at least 5 adult volunteers. Measure the length from each person's elbow to the tip of her or his middle finger in centimetres.
Record the measurements in a table.

Name	Length from elbow to tip of finger (cm)

2 Determine the median of the lengths in your table. You will use this as your "official" cubit. Get a piece of string. Make marks on the string at intervals equal to your official cubit. You now have created a cubit measuring tape!

3 **a.** Use your cubit measuring tape. Measure the length of your desk, your classroom,

and at least three other objects in your school or schoolyard. You might need to estimate fractional parts of a cubit for some items. Measure each item with a metric measuring tape as well. Record both measurements in a table.

Item	Length (cubits)	Length (m or cm)

b. Compare your measurements with those of other students who measured the same objects. Which were closer, the lengths in cubits or in metric units? Why do you think this is the case?

4 Here are the metric equivalents of the cubits used by some ancient cultures. How do they compare with your "official" cubit?

Culture	Length of cubit (cm)
Babylonian	52.8
Egyptian	52.4
Hebrew	52.5
Greek	46.3
Roman	44.4

DESIGN
A Dream School

Here is your chance
to design the school of your dreams.
You are the architect. Money is not
an issue. Include everything
you think the ideal school
should have.

Work with your group to plan
your dream school. Draw a floor plan
of the school and a plan
of the playground.
Include all dimensions on
your plans. Make sure your plans
meet the design guidelines
on page 287.

Write to describe your school design.
Explain how you used the ideas
of area and perimeter in your plans.

School Design Guidelines

1   Your school must be situated on one hectare of land.
    (1 ha = 10 000 m²)

2   Your school must include:
    • a minimum of six classrooms
    • a regulation-size gym (30 m by 20 m)
    • washrooms
    • offices

3   Each classroom must have an area of 60 m².

4   Your school may have any other features you like;
    for example, a greenhouse, a swimming pool,
    a computer room, a tennis court, and so on.

*Check***Y**OURSELF

Great Job! Your school design is complete. You
included all the dimensions and you followed all the
guidelines. You wrote to explain how you used
perimeter and area in your plans.

PROBLEM BANK

1. Draw each figure with a perimeter of 20 cm.
   - rectangle
   - square
   - regular pentagon

2. The perimeter of a rectangle is 90 mm. The length is twice as long as the width. Find the dimensions of the rectangle.

3. Find the perimeter of each polygon. Write an expression to show how you found each perimeter.

   a.   **b.**   **c.**   **d.**

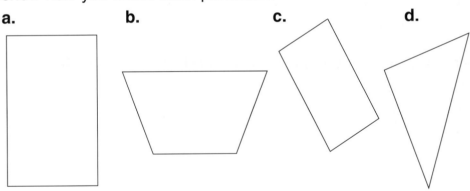

4. A pentagon has sides measuring 65 cm, 1.0 m, 1.5 m, 73 cm, and 76 cm. What is its perimeter?

5. A square has a perimeter of 3 m. What is the length of each side?

6. Draw a square and a rectangle that is not a square with the same area.

7. Find the perimeter and area of each item.

8. Suppose you double the length of each side of a square. Explain what happens to its area.

9. Funland Amusement Park covers an area of 12 km². The park is rectangular. What might its length and width be? Find as many solutions as you can.

10. Use a copy of 1-cm grid paper. Draw and label a model of each sports area using the information in the chart. Copy and complete the chart.

	Length	**Width**	**Area**
Soccer	?	45 m	4050 m²
Hockey	60 m	30 m	?
Tennis	?	20 m	600 m²
Basketball	?	14 m	364 m²
Football	145 m	?	7250 m²

11. Peggy's garden has an area of 120 m². What might the length and width of the garden be? Which dimensions give the shortest perimeter?

12. A rectangle has a length 3 cm greater than its width. Its area is 54 cm². What are its length and width?

1. Find the perimeter of each figure.

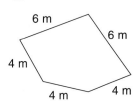

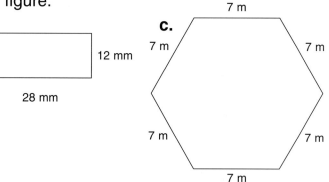

2. For each perimeter, draw two different polygons.

    a. 8 cm   **b.** 16 cm   **c.** 20 cm

3. Find the area of each rectangle.

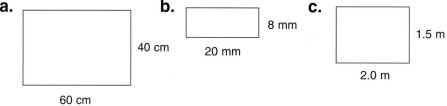

4. For each area, draw two different rectangles.

    a. 18 cm²   **b.** 30 cm²   **c.** 36 cm²

5. Draw a rectangle with perimeter 36 cm and the least possible area.

6. Draw a rectangle with area 40 cm² and the greatest possible perimeter.

7. a. Draw a rectangle with area 27 cm².
    b. What is its perimeter?
    c. Draw a different rectangle with the same perimeter.
    d. What is the area of the rectangle in part c?

1. What solid can be made from each net?

a. 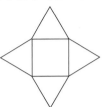   **b.**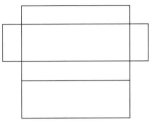

2. How many faces does each solid have?

a. 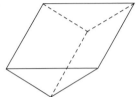   **b.** 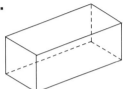   **c.**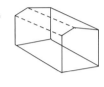

3. Copy and complete the chart. Each box is a rectangular prism.

	Length (cm)	Width (cm)	Height (cm)	Volume (cm³)	Surface Area (cm²)
Box A	20	15	10	?	?
Box B	11	5	?	550	?

4. a. Someone can choose one item from each section of the lunch menu. What different lunch combinations could the person choose?

Soups	Sandwiches	Sundaes
chicken	roast beef	chocolate
vegetable	tuna	strawberry
	egg salad	

b. Suppose the choice is random. What is the probability of choosing chicken soup, an egg salad sandwich, and a chocolate sundae?

5. Copy and complete each pair of equivalent fractions.

a. $\frac{1}{6} = \frac{\blacksquare}{48}$ **b.** $\frac{1}{8} = \frac{\blacksquare}{40}$ **c.** $\frac{3}{4} = \frac{\blacksquare}{60}$ **d.** $\frac{2}{5} = \frac{\blacksquare}{50}$

6. Suppose you rolled a cube numbered 1, 1, 2, 3, 4, 5. What would be the probability of obtaining each outcome?

a. a 3   **b.** a 4   **c.** a number less than 3

d. an even number   **e.** a 6

Index

Acknowledgments

ILLUSTRATION

Cover Illustration: **Seymour Chwast**
Clarence Porter: 8, 9, 10–11; **Mario Pia Marrella:** 12–15; **Greg Valley:** 16–18; **Steve Sullivan:** 17, 18; **Dale Verzaal:** 22–25; **Brian Callanan:** 26, 27; **Clarence Porter:** 33; **Jere Smith:** 43–45; **Ken Bowser:** 46–47; **Robert Dales:** 48–49; **Clarence Porter:** 62–63; **Peter Cook:** 64, 65; **Renée Mansfield:** 66, 67, 68; **David Diaz:** 71; **Lisa Henderling:** 72–74; **Obadinah Heavner:** 77, 78; **Peter Cook:** 80, 81; **Anne Neumann:** 84–85; **Clarence Porter:** 92; **Doug Panton:** 93; **Stephen Taylor:** 94; **Peter Cook:** 95; **Peter Cook:** 102–103; **R.M. Schneider:** 104–105; **Tadeusz Majewski:** 115; **Don Kilby:** 126–127; **Robert Johannsen:** 128–129; **Alan Mazzetti:** 130; **Clarence Porter:** 131, 132; **Neil Shigley:** 134–135; **Don Kilby:** 142; **Scott Ritchie:** 148–149; **Don Kilby:** 154; **Steve Sullivan:** 158, 159, 160; **Don Kilby:** 161; **Clarence Porter:** 164; **Paragraphics:** 165, 166–167; **Frank Hammond:** 180–181; **Vesna Krstanovich:** 182–183; **Mike Reagan:** 186–187; **Roberta Ludlow:** 188–189; **Roger Chandler:** 190–191; **Amy Bryant:** 192–193; **Clarence Porter:** 200; **Teco Rodrigues:** 201; **Brian Deines:** 206–207; **Teco Rodrigues:** 208–209; **Peter Cook:** 210, 211, 213; **Teco Rodrigues:** 216, 217; **Peter Cook:** 228; **Rebecca Ruegger:** 230–231; **Michael McParlane:** 250–251; **Barbara Spurll:** 253; **Clarence Porter:** 260-261; **Peter Cook:** 262; **Jewell Homad:** 264–265; **Brnadette Lau:** 268, 270; **Teco Rodrigues:** 269; **Clarence Porter:** 274–275; **Teco Rodrigues:** 276; **Tadeusz Majewski:** 278, 281; **Clarence Porter:** 289.

PHOTOGRAPHY

Photo Management: **Nancy Haffner;** Picture Research: **Photosearch, Inc.**
Everett Studios: 6–7; **Claire Aich:** 12–15, 18; **Everett Studios:** 28–29, 35; **Ian Crysler:** 34–35; **Wada/Gamma, Pono Press Internationale:** 36; **Animals, Animals:** 38, 39; **Ken Karp:** 40, 41; **Garcia Arnal/Retna Ltd.:** 42; **Stephen J. Krasemann/Photo Researchers:** 48 left; **H. Uible/Photo Researchers:** 48 right; **Dr. Tony Brain/ Photo Researchers:** 50 bottom left; **Dr. Jeremy Burgess/Photo Researchers:** 50 middle; **A. B. Dowsett/Photo Researchers:** 50 top left; **Professor P. Motta/Photo Researchers:** 50-51 top; **John Walsh/Photo Researchers:** 50-51 bottom; **Claire Aich:** 52–53; **Everett Studios:** 54–55; **Jean Kugler/FPG:** 54–55 left; **Erik Schnakenberg/ Leo de Wys:** 55 right; **Belinda Wright/DRK Photo:** 57; **Ken Karp:** 60–61; **Claire Aich:** 75, 76, 79, 82–85; **John Lei:** 86; **Ken Karp:** 90–91; **Claire Aich:** 98–99; **Ian Crysler:** 100–101; **Claire Aich:** 104–107; **Richard Simpson/ Tony Stone Images:** 108–109; **R. Krubner/H. Armstrong Roberts:** 110; **Claire Aich:** 116–117; **Ian Crysler:** 124–125; **Everett Studios, Robert Llewellyn:** 124–125; **Richard Hutchings:** 138, 139; **Everett Studios:** 140–141; **Everett Studios:** 146–147; **Richard Hutchings:** 152; **Ian Crysler:** 153; **Richard Hutchings:** 156, 157; **Everett Studios:** 168–169; **Ian Crysler:** 176–177; **John Edwards/Tony Stone Images:** 178–179; **Claire Aich:** 184–185, 190; **Photo Researchers:** 194; **Ian Crysler:** 196–200; **Dave Starrett Photographer:** 204–205; **Ian Crysler:** 210, 211, 212, 214; **Dave Starrett Photographer:** 218–219; **Fred McConnaughey/Photo Researchers (all four):** 223; **Claire Aich:** 224–225; **John Lamb/Tony Stone Images:** 226–227; **Ian Crysler:** 233, 237; **Claire Aich:** 238–239; **Claire Aich:** 242–243, 248–249; **Ian Crysler:** 252, 254, 255, 257; **Richard Hutchings:** 263; **Claire Aich, Ian Crysler:** 266–267; **Ian Crysler:** 268; **Dave Starrett Photographer:** 272–273; **Ian Crysler:** 282; **Dave Starrett Photographer:** 286–287.